PANINI, BRUSCHETTA, CROSTINI

VIANA LA PLACE

panini

crostini bruschetta

sandwiches, italian style

PHOTOGRAPHS BY MARIA ROBLEDO

WM

WILLIAM MORROW
An Imprint of HarperCollins Publishers

PANINI, BRUSCHETTA, CROSTINI. Copyright © 1994 by Viana La Place. All rights
reserved. Manufactured in China . No part of this book may be used or reproduced in any
manner whatsoever without written permission except in the case of brief quotations
embodied in critical articles and reviews. For information address HarperCollins
Publishers Inc., 10 East 53rd Street, New York, NY 10022.

HarperCollins books may be purchased for educational, business, or sales promotional
use. For information please write: Special Markets Department, HarperCollins
Publishers Inc., 10 East 53rd Street, New York, NY 10022.

First William Morrow paperback edition published 2002

Designed by Ph.D
Illustrations copyright © 1994 by Ann Field
Photographs copyright © 1994 by Maria Robledo
Food styling by Susan Spungen

The Library of Congress has catalogued the hardcover edition as follows:
La Place, Viana
    Panini, bruschetta, crostini : sandwiches, Italian style / Viana
La Place
      p. cm.
    Includes index.
    ISBN 0-688-11325-7
    1. Sandwiches. 2. Cookery, Italian. I. Title
TX818.L3 1994
641.8'4'0945—dc20   93-39917
                                   CIP

Manufactured in China.

ISBN 0-06-009572-5 (pbk.)

08 // 11 12 13 14 15 16 17 18 19 20

Acknowledgments

I feel incredibly fortunate to have as my colleagues on this book the most talented people in their fields.

To Maria Robledo, thank you for your transcendent photographs. Your photography—its integrity and simplicity—perfectly reflects my own philosophy about food. I couldn't imagine doing this book with anyone else.

To Susan Spungen, a food stylist with a sure eye and hand, thank you for bringing your love of food and your wonderful energy to this project. And thanks for gathering the best and freshest ingredients, including smoked mozzarella from Joe's Dairy and a mountain of incredible bread, and bringing it into the studio.

To Clive Piercy, a grateful thank you for your dedication to this project, for putting it all together and making it look so beautiful. And a special thank you for making my writing big.

To Ann Field, thank you for your warm support and delightful drawings.

To Sonia Greenbaum, many, many thanks for your informed and insightful copyediting.

How can I express my gratitude to my editor, Ann Bramson, for believing in me and encouraging me all these years? To Ann, a big, heartfelt thank you.

And loving thanks to my mother, Antonietta La Place, whose stories about life in Italy are a continual source of delight and inspiration.

5

Bread is basic to the way Italians eat, so it is not surprising that they have devised a variety of ways to enjoy it. Not only does bread always accompany a meal, but the Italian repertoire includes numerous dishes in which it plays an important role. In *Panini, Bruschetta, Crostini,* I explore three variations on the theme of bread: panini, Italian-style sandwiches; bruschetta, grilled bread with toppings, a kind of rustic open-faced sandwich; and crostini, miniature, sophisticated versions of bruschetta.

Panini means rolls or little breads. In Italy the word is synonymous with sandwiches. Prepared with care and creativity, panini feature the type of fresh and healthy ingredients we have come to associate with Italian cooking.

In the book, you'll find recipes for crusty rolls spread with crushed black olives and stuffed with artichokes and tuna; rosemary-scented chicken and sweet peppers layered between slices of grilled country bread; warm focaccia panini filled with ricotta and sautéed greens; and delicate tramezzini with smoked salmon. Have you ever considered making a sweet sandwich? Try a toasted bittersweet chocolate sandwich or a marmalade frittata layered between slices of chewy bread!

In America, panini are catching on and putting a whole new spin on the art of sandwich making.

In a panino, bread encloses the ingredients. Bruschetta is the foundation for toppings. At its most basic, bruschetta is a thick slice of crusty country bread, grilled, then rubbed while still hot with garlic and drizzled with fruity olive oil. (Our garlic bread derives from this rustic dish.) Bruschetta can also become the base for a wide selection of savory toppings and be served as an antipasto, first course, main dish, or afternoon snack. Rough vegetable purees, white beans infused with the fragrance of herbs, coarsely mashed avocado seasoned with oregano and capers—all are equally at home atop slices of warm, fragrant grilled bread. Bruschetta can also be used to create country desserts or sweet snacks. You'll find recipes for bread, minus the olive oil and garlic, topped with fruits or spread with fresh dessert cheeses.

Crostini are diminutive, more refined versions of bruschetta, like an Italian-style canape. Small rounds or squares of toasted bread boast toppings that range from diced summer tomatoes to rich goat cheese spreads. Served as an antipasto, crostini make perfect party food since they can be eaten with the fingers. And yes, there are even recipes for dessert crostini—imagine little circles of bread spread with mocha-flavored cream or with a topping of Italian cream cheese and juicy marinated cherries.

One of the great charms of the recipes in *Panini, Bruschetta, Crostini* is their simplicity. From crostini for a large gathering, to bruschetta served at the beginning of a rustic dinner, to elegant tea sandwiches, the recipes require relatively little effort. In fact, they are downright fun to prepare. Time required at the stove is a bare minimum and many of the recipes require no cooking at all! Just assemble the best and freshest ingredients you can find.

Good bread is crucial to the success of the recipes. It must be the best bread available, either purchased from a high-quality bread bakery or made at home. Now we are discovering what Italians have known all along—that bread is a complete and nourishing food that should assume a more important role in our diets. When bread is made from healthy grains and fiber, it can be fully enjoyed without guilt. And when bread is combined with ingredients such as fresh mozzarella, creamy gorgonzola, rosy prosciutto, sweet-smelling basil leaves and pungent oregano, brilliantly colored peppers, and glossy black olives—the results are exciting.

Most of the recipes in the book take their inspiration from Italy rather than being traditional or from a specific region, although a few are both time-honored and regional. I encourage you to have fun with this book and bring your own creativity to making panini, bruschetta, and crostini. I guarantee you'll never think of sandwiches in the same way again, and when you discover the world of panini, bruschetta, and crostini, you'll make them as intrinsic to your repertoire as they are to mine.

11

Americans are rediscovering the importance of bread, how wholesome and nutritious it is, and leaving behind the fallacious notion that bread is a fattening, empty food to be avoided. Quality bread bakeries are helping to change that old view of bread which was based on a factory-made version that desecrates the very idea of what bread should be: a whole food that can sustain life. That "false" bread—wrapped in colorful, shiny packaging, its texture soft as a marshmallow, and containing about as much nutrition—really deserves to be avoided.

Now, new high-quality bakeries are producing real bread, the kind that had become a distant memory. Even supermarkets are responding to consumer demand by making available breads that contain whole grains, free of preservatives and other harmful additives. Still, even an improved factory-produced bread invariably lacks the crust, the body, the flavor, the nutrition, the soul of bread produced by small, artisan-style bakeries, which is the kind I recommend that you use for the recipes in this book.

People who make their own bread know the special satisfaction of a homemade loaf—the satiny feel of the dough when kneaded, the smell of the yeast, the miracle of the dough doubling and tripling in size, the aroma of the finished bread when it comes out of the oven, brown and crusty, and the hollow sound the bottom of the loaf makes when tested for doneness. If you already bake, but want to learn the specifics of baking Italian breads, or if you are a beginner, Carol Field's *The Italian Baker* is the definitive guide to Italian bread baking.

Good bread should be available to everyone, every day. Italian towns, no matter how small, have at least one *panificio*, a bakery devoted exclusively to bread. In larger towns and cities there seems to be one around every corner, each featuring its specialties—crusty little rolls shaped like artichokes, flat breads sprinkled with sparkling sea salt, big round loaves baked to a deep brown with a coarse golden-yellow crumb—indigenous to that particular town or region. Today in Italy, whole grain breads are becoming more and more popular, as Italians themselves rediscover their own earliest traditions.

I strongly urge you to support and encourage the new artisan-style bakeries that are springing up across the United States. While major cities may be able to support a number of high-quality bread bakeries, small towns or cities might discover that the best bread available is in their ethnic markets. It is up to us to seek out and acknowledge those bakers who dedicate themselves passionately to this noble endeavor; in return we will receive nourishment to feed the body and soul.

on bread

PANINI PARTY EXTRAVAGANZA
Panini alla Norma
Goat Cheese and Roasted Pepper Panini
Panini di Prosciutto e Mozzarella
Chicken and Salsa Verde Panini
Focaccia with Sautéed Mushrooms
Miniature cannoli* and bowls of fresh cherries*
Hazelnut, chocolate, and espresso gelato*
Wine, beer, Italian sodas, and mineral water

AFTERNOON TEA, ITALIAN STYLE
Avocado, Caper, and Arugula Tramezzini
Chicken Tramezzini with Lemon Butter
Insalata Russa and Shrimp Tramezzini
Miniature Herb Frittata Panini
Crostini with Mascarpone and Cherries
Aperitifs, white wine, and assorted teas

CROSTINI PARTY FOR A CROWD
Avocado and Goat Cheese Crostini
Crostini with Black Olive Pesto
Crostini with Savory Mushroom Topping
Crostini alla Checca
Polenta Triangles with Peppers and Gorgonzola
Baskets of pinzimonio (tender raw vegetables)
with extra-virgin olive oil dipping sauce*
Assorted wines and mineral waters

SUMMER GRILL PICNIC
Bruschetta with Ammogghiu Sauce
Panini di Verdura alla Griglia
Marinated Mushrooms
Grilled fruits* and amaretti cookies*
Red wine and mineral water

*Asterisks mark simple recipes or foods not included in this book

CHILDREN'S LUNCH PARTY
Crostini alla Pizzaiola
Orange Marmalade Frittata Panini
Fruit Salad*
Italian sodas and fruit juices

RUSTIC BRUSCHETTA BUFFET
Bruschetta with Arugula Salad
Sweet Pepper Bruschetta
Bruschetta con Frutti di Mare
Platter of Prosciutto*
Tomato and Mozzarella Salad*
Fresh figs* and anise cookies*
Red wine

BRUNCH IN THE GARDEN
Crostini Topped with Scrambled Eggs, Italian Style
Bruschetta al Prosciutto served with fresh figs
Bruschetta con Ricotta Fresca served with black olives
Salad of tender lettuces and nasturtiums*
Nectarines*
Fresh mixed citrus juice and cappuccino

ROMAN PANINI PARTY
Fontina "Toast"
4-Seasons Pizza Romana
Tuna and Artichoke Panini
Rosemary Focaccia with Ricotta and Swiss Chard
Dishes of small green olives*
White wine, Italian beer, iced tea, and imported mineral water

REFINED LITTLE COCKTAIL PARTY
Black and White Tramezzini
Whole Grain Tramezzini with Smoked Salmon
Panini di Polenta Dorata
Campari and soda, vermouth, champagne, and imported mineral water

*Asterisks mark simple recipes or foods not included in this book

Panini: Sandwiches, Italian Style

Although the Earl of Sandwich is credited with creating the sandwich in eighteenth-century England, bread has been a part of Italian eating traditions since Roman times. In a country that venerates bread, the marriage of bread and filling was preordained.

From the skilled hands of the Italian bread baker comes a range of wonderful breads to choose from: rolls such as michette, hollow in the middle, or rosette, shaped like roses; hearty cigar-shaped loaves, called filone; and huge wheels of chewy country bread. These, and many similar breads, become the foundation for panini.

Panini have become part of the snacking tradition in Italy to be savored as a light bite between meals, miniature panini served with drinks before dinner, panini tucked into a basket to be eaten on a picnic or on the train. Although having a panino for lunch at one time went against tradition, even in Italy, the land of the long lunch, modern life has started to change some of those customs. At midday, *caffès* and bars are crowded with busy working people enjoying freshly made panini they have chosen from an appetizing display.

The following recipes reflect the spirit of Italian panini. I've tried to stay true to Italian simplicity and freshness by pairing just a few major ingredients in each sandwich—dripping fresh mozzarella and sweet, salty prosciutto; thickly sliced summer tomatoes and heady garden herbs; lush sautéed peppers and creamy goat cheese—to highlight rather than hide their flavor. For contrast there are pungent olives and capers, fruity sun-dried tomatoes, peppery arugula leaves, aromatic lemon juice and vinegar, and creamy lemon mayonnaise, for a touch of richness or a burst of flavor.

If authentic Italian-style breads are not available, any high quality bread can be used—just select one that approximates the type of bread called for in the recipe. The other ingredients are easily found at Italian markets, specialty food shops, and at your local supermarket.

18

Country-Style Tomato Panino

What could be more refreshing on a hot summer day than a panino filled with cool, juicy slices of tart-sweet tomato and fragrant herbs? When the tomatoes are layered between slices of rustic bread, the panino satisfies as well as refreshes.

2 slices Italian-style whole grain bread

Extra-virgin olive oil

Fresh lemon juice or imported red wine vinegar

Salt and freshly ground black pepper

Chopped basil and mint leaves

Pinch dried Mediterranean oregano, such as Greek oregano

Touch of finely chopped garlic

1 medium ripe but firm tomato, cored and sliced

Drizzle 1 side of both slices of bread with olive oil and lemon juice or vinegar. Season with salt and pepper. Scatter some herbs and garlic over 1 slice of bread. Top with the sliced tomato. Season with more salt and pepper and another scattering of herbs and garlic. Cover with the other slice of bread.

Makes 1 panino.

19

Umbrian Black Olive Panino

A panino for those who can make a meal of bread and olives. Serve with a cool glass of pure water or a good glass of red wine.

Select plump, glossy, pleasingly pungent black olives. Taste one first before buying—the flavor should be strong but not excessively sharp or salty, and the flesh should be moist.

1 small crusty roll, with a firm, chewy crumb

1 garlic clove, peeled

Extra-virgin olive oil

Juice of ½ a small lemon

About 8 oil-cured black olives, pitted, cut in half

1 teaspoon orange zest, preferably from an organic orange (use a zester to create thin strips)

Slice the roll in half horizontally. Pull out a little of the inside of the bread to form shallow hollows. Cut the garlic clove in half. Rub the inside of both halves of the bread with the cut garlic clove. You can determine how much garlic flavor you want by how hard you rub the clove into the bread. Drizzle the bread generously with olive oil and lemon juice. Nestle the olives into the bottom half of the roll, sprinkle with orange zest, and cover with the other half.

Makes 1 panino.

20

Panini del Giardino

I love radishes. Their leafy green tops and rosy color make me think of spring and the carefully tended kitchen gardens that are an integral part of the Italian landscape.

The following panino is inspired by those spring gardens. Use your very best rustic Italian bread, coarse and nutty tasting. Select small to medium-sized radishes that are very firm to the touch and have fresh foliage.

1 small bunch radishes

Unsalted butter, slightly softened at room temperature

4 slices rustic whole grain bread

Salt and freshly ground black pepper

Handful mixed mild baby lettuces

Trim the radishes and thinly slice them. Generously butter bread. Place half of the radishes on 2 slices of bread. Season liberally with salt and pepper. Top with a generous scattering of lettuce leaves. Arrange the remaining radishes over the lettuces and cover with the other 2 slices of buttered bread.

Makes 2 panini.

22

Pan Bagna

The name of this sandwich from the south of France, which means moistened or soaked bread, refers to the generous amount of olive oil drizzled on it. The very Italian-sounding name harks back to a time when sections of southern France were, in fact, part of Italy.

Layered with fresh vegetables and tangy condiments, the panino is compressed with a weight (a heavy can or pot), which encourages the ingredients to hold together and the flavors to merge. This panino is ideal for a picnic. I can imagine eating it under a shady pine tree on a summer day by the sea.

4 crusty sandwich rolls with a sturdy, coarse crumb

2 garlic cloves, peeled and cut in half

Extra-virgin olive oil

Coarsely chopped basil and mint leaves

2 ripe but firm medium tomatoes, sliced

8 oil-cured black olives, pitted

2 teaspoons capers

1 sweet yellow pepper, cored, seeded, membranes removed, and sliced into thin rounds

Handful peeled tender fava beans

Imported red wine vinegar

Salt and freshly ground black pepper

Cut the rolls in half lengthwise. Rub with the cut sides of the garlic cloves and drizzle with olive oil. Layer the remaining ingredients on the bottom half of the rolls in the order listed. Drizzle with olive oil and vinegar. Season with salt and pepper to taste. Cover with the top half of the rolls. Place a weight on top of the panini and remove after about 30 minutes.

Makes 4 panini.

23

Panini di Verdura alla Griglia

Grilling brings out the sweetness of the vegetables while infusing them with a smoky perfume.

When it's not convenient to fire up the barbecue, I grill food on the stove, with a cast-iron stovetop grill I bought in Italy many years ago. I strongly encourage you to make the small investment required to purchase a good quality, hinged cast-iron stovetop grill, available in specialty kitchenware shops in this country. It lasts forever and allows you to grill foods whenever you get the urge.

1 firm green zucchini, about 5 inches long

2 small plump Japanese eggplants

1 small red onion

Extra-virgin olive oil

1 medium fully ripe red bell pepper

1 small garlic clove, peeled and finely chopped

1 teaspoon chopped thyme

4 large thin slices country bread

Black Olive Pesto (see page 106)

Trim the zucchini and slice it lengthwise into ¼-inch slices. Trim the tops of the eggplants and slice lengthwise into ¼-inch slices. Trim and peel the red onion, and slice thickly through the root end. Lightly brush the sliced vegetables with olive oil and grill over an outdoor grill or stovetop grill until tender.

Roast the red pepper over the grill. When it is charred all over, but before any gray ash has formed, put the pepper into a brown paper bag and twist the top closed. After about 15 minutes, remove the pepper and peel it without using water, which washes away some of the syrupy juices on the surface. Use a paper towel to wipe away charred pieces of skin. Cut the pepper in half and remove the core, membranes, and seeds. Cut the flesh into thick strips.

Place all the prepared vegetables in a shallow bowl and sprinkle with the chopped garlic and thyme. If vegetables are dry-looking, drizzle with a little olive oil. The vegetables can be prepared several hours in advance of assembling the panini.

Lightly grill the bread slices on both sides. Spread 2 of the slices with a little black olive pesto. Arrange the vegetables over the olive pesto. Drizzle with any juices remaining in the bowl. Cover with the remaining bread slices.

Makes 2 large panini.

Panini Caprese

A classic southern Italian salad called caprese combines fresh white mozzarella, sliced tomatoes, and basil. Here, the same ingredients bring the feeling of summer in Italy to a panino. An added touch is a sprinkling of aromatic dried oregano, an herb at home in the sun-baked Italian south.

Fresh mozzarella is packed in water to maintain its moisture. Drain the cheese and place it on several layers of tea towels to absorb excess water.

I like to grill the inside of the bread lightly, which keeps the panini crisp.

1 large ball fresh mozzarella, about ½ pound

2 large rolls, round or baguette shaped

Extra-virgin olive oil

2 medium tomatoes, ripe but firm, cored and sliced

Salt and freshly ground black pepper to taste

Dried Mediterranean oregano, such as Greek oregano

8 basil leaves

Cut the mozzarella in slices and place on folded clean tea towels. Meanwhile, slice the rolls in half horizontally. Place bread cut side down on a grill or cut side up under a hot broiler, until lightly toasted. Drizzle both sides of the bread with olive oil.

Arrange tomatoes on bottom halves of rolls. Season with salt and pepper, a sprinkling of oregano, and a drizzle of olive oil. Arrange the mozzarella on top of the tomatoes. Season again with salt, pepper, oregano, and olive oil. Top with the whole basil leaves. Cover with the top halves of the rolls.

Makes 2 panini.

25

Panini with Gorgonzola and Greens

Here, a salad of greens, Gorgonzola, croutons, and dressing is transformed into a panino.

The recipe calls for a combination of endive, escarole, and radicchio, but you can use any mix of crisp, tangy salad greens. Dressed with olive oil and vinegar, the greens top bread spread with Gorgonzola.

Look for imported *dolce latte* Gorgonzola; it is buttery, creamy, and a little funky all at the same time.

½ cup each thinly sliced escarole, endive, and radicchio

1 tablespoon extra-virgin olive oil

2 teaspoons imported red wine vinegar

Salt and freshly ground black pepper

4 slices crusty country bread, white or mild whole wheat

2 ounces Gorgonzola, softened at room temperature

Place the greens in a small bowl and dress with the oil, vinegar, and salt and pepper to taste. Remember that the Gorgonzola is salty, so go easy on the salt. Toss well.

Spread 2 slices of bread with Gorgonzola. Top with the greens and drizzle with any dressing left in the bowl. Cover with the remaining bread and press down lightly.

Makes 2 panini.

Panini alla Norma

Pasta with eggplant, tomato, salted ricotta, and basil, called Pasta alla Norma, is one of my all-time favorites. Claimed by the city of Catania, the pasta is named in honor of a masterwork by its famous native son, the composer Vincenzo Bellini.

I've used the same ingredients (minus the pasta!) in a sublime sandwich.that does justice to its namesake. Although tradition calls for grated dry ricotta salata, moist ricotta salata gives the sandwich a tangy, creamy quality. If unavailable, substitute feta cheese.

Ciabatta means "slipper" and this bread, with its elongated, flattened shape, does indeed resemble bedroom slippers. Any chewy, crusty flatbread can be used instead.

1 pound firm, shiny eggplant, either Japanese or regular globe-shaped

Salt

Extra-virgin olive oil

4 large pieces ciabatta, each 5 × 4 inches, or 4 slices crusty flatbread

¼ cup Basil Pesto Spread (see page 29)

2 tablespoons coarsely chopped walnuts

1 large ripe but firm tomato, cored and cut into 8 slices

4 ounces moist ricotta salata, coarsely crumbled

8 large fresh basil leaves

Trim the tops of the eggplant. Slice lengthwise about ¼ inch thick. If time permits, salt slices lightly and let drain for 30 minutes. Wipe dry. Brush eggplant on both sides with olive oil. Arrange the eggplant slices on a baking sheet. Bake at 400° for about 10 minutes. Turn slices over and brush with more olive oil if slices appear dry. Cook about another 10 minutes, or until the eggplant is tender and lightly golden. Remove from oven and blot off excess oil with paper towels.

Slice the bread in half horizontally. Toast lightly to crisp bread. Spread half the pesto on the 4 bottom slices of bread. Sprinkle with walnuts. Layer eggplant slices over the pesto. Top with tomato slices, crumbled ricotta salata, and whole basil leaves. Spread remaining pesto on the other bread slices. Cover and press down lightly.

Makes 4 panini.

28

Basil Pesto Spread

Fresh basil pesto led the revolution in authentic Italian cooking in America. It wasn't red and it didn't cook for hours on the stove. In fact, it was green! And you didn't have to cook it at all! The fragrant green leaves, crushed with garlic and pine nuts, when tossed with freshly cooked pasta, creates a dish of unforgettable aroma and taste.

Aromatic pesto can be used as a spread for panini with equally memorable effect. The following recipe produces a dense mixture specifically for panini; to use with pasta, just add a little more olive oil and thin with some hot pasta cooking water.

2 cups bright green aromatic basil leaves, tightly packed

⅓ cup extra-virgin olive oil

2 fresh white garlic cloves, peeled and crushed (use a mortar and pestle)

¼ cup pine nuts, coarsely crushed (use a mortar and pestle)

Salt

3 tablespoons freshly grated imported Parmesan cheese

4 tablespoons freshly grated imported Pecorino Romano cheese

Place basil, olive oil, garlic, pine nuts, and salt to taste in a blender. Process until finely textured but not completely smooth. Scrape pesto into a bowl and stir in the cheeses. If not using immediately, pour a thin layer of extra-virgin olive oil over the top. Wrap tightly and refrigerate until needed.

Makes about 1 cup.

29

Goat Cheese and Roasted Pepper Panini

Tart goat cheese, aromatic herbs, and roasted sweet peppers are an irresistible taste combination. The chalk white goat cheese flecked with green herbs contrasts beautifully with the bright red peppers.

5½ ounces goat cheese, softened at room temperature

3 green onions, trimmed of half of the green tops, finely chopped

1 tablespoon chopped Italian parsley

1 tablespoon chopped basil

1 small garlic clove, peeled and finely chopped

Salt and freshly ground black pepper

2 ripe red bell peppers

2 tablespoons extra-virgin olive oil

2 tablespoons lemon juice

2 tablespoons capers

Small pinch hot red pepper flakes

4 michette, or round rolls, about 5 inches in diameter

If time permits, roast and marinate the peppers a few hours before using. These luscious peppers are also delicious served alongside panini.

Place the goat cheese in a bowl and combine with the green onions, herbs and garlic. Season with salt and pepper. Set aside. You can prepare cheese mixture several hours in advance. Refrigerate, then bring to room temperature before using.

Roast the peppers. Remove the blackened skin, core, seeds, and membranes. Cut into thick strips. Place on a plate and toss in olive oil, lemon juice, capers, and hot red pepper flakes. Season with salt and pepper.

Split the rolls in half. Spread the goat cheese on the bottom half of the rolls. Top with strips of roasted peppers and capers. Drizzle the remaining juices over the inside of the top half of the rolls. Cover panini with the top halves.

Makes 4 panini.

Big Loaf with Pinzimonio

The most tender vegetables of the season, when served raw with an olive oil dipping sauce, are called pinzimonio. Here, a garden's worth of raw vegetables are layered over fresh mozzarella, each ingredient bathed in olive oil and lemon juice. The sandwich looks fresh and inviting, like a salad within a sandwich.

For an alfresco lunch, present the loaf unsliced, then cut into sections at the table. Serve with oil-cured black olives flavored with red pepper flakes. Offer Italian soft drinks such as aranciata and chinotto, and a big bottle of mineral water. For dessert—a bowl of seasonal fruits cooled with ice cubes.

1 flat loaf country bread, such as ciabatta

Extra-virgin olive oil

Lemon juice

Salt and freshly ground black pepper

4 big, very green leaves of butter lettuce

½ pound fresh mozzarella, drained and thinly sliced

4 Roma tomatoes, cored and sliced

1 small red onion, thinly sliced

1 yellow sweet pepper, cored and seeded, cut into thin rounds

2 sweet carrots, peeled and thinly sliced

6 radishes, trimmed and thinly sliced

10 basil leaves

Cut bread in half horizontally. If the loaf is more than a couple of inches thick, pull out some of the soft bread in the top and bottom to create hollows. Moisten interior of both halves generously with olive oil and lemon juice and season with salt and pepper.

Layer the rest of the ingredients on the bottom half of the bread in the order listed. Drizzle each layer with a few drops of olive oil and lemon juice and season with salt and pepper. Cover with the top half of the loaf. Press down lightly to hold ingredients together.

Keep loaf whole for presentation. Right before serving, cut into 4 sections.

Makes 4 panini.

Panino di Prosciutto e Mozzarella

Velvety-pink prosciutto and mild, milky-white mozzarella are tucked into this classic panino. For years we had to make do with second-rate versions of both. It is only recently that fresh mozzarella in water has become more widely available; even more recent is the appearance of authentic Italian prosciutto in our markets.

Use prosciutto imported from Parma, Italy. It is expensive but exquisite, and a little goes a long way. Also, it is free of preservatives.

Bocconcini, little mouthfuls, are small balls of fresh mozzarella. They are generally available wherever fresh mozzarella is sold. You can substitute an equal weight of fresh mozzarella sliced from a large round.

1 large sturdy baguette-shaped roll

4–5 slices imported Italian prosciutto, about ⅛ pound

2 ounces fresh bocconcini, thickly sliced, drained on tea towels

Extra-virgin olive oil

Freshly ground black pepper

4 whole basil leaves

Cut the roll in half horizontally. Arrange the prosciutto on the bottom half of the roll. Top the prosciutto with the sliced mozzarella. Drizzle a few drops of olive oil over the cheese and grind black pepper on top. Arrange the basil leaves over the cheese and cover with the top of the roll.

Makes 1 big panino.

34

Panino with Bresaola, Robiola, and Arugula

Many high-quality gourmet shops or stores that stock a wide range of imported Italian foods carry bresaola.

Dark and tangy, bresaola is beef fillet cured in salt and air-dried. It is sliced very thinly and often served as an appetizer. Since bresaola dries out quickly after slicing, plan to use it no longer than 24 hours after purchase.

Robiola, a soft, white cheese from Piedmont, may be hard to find. If unavailable, mild fresh goat cheese makes an excellent substitute.

1 large baguette-shaped roll

2 ounces robiola

Extra-virgin olive oil

5 slices bresaola

Freshly ground black pepper

3 arugula leaves, stems trimmed

Slice the roll in half lengthwise. Spread the robiola on one half of the bread. Drizzle with a few drops of olive oil. Layer the bresaola over the cheese. Grind black pepper over the meat. Arrange a few arugula leaves over the bresaola. Drizzle lightly with olive oil. Cover with the other slice of bread.

Makes 1 panino.

Chicken and Salsa Verde Panini

Salsa verde is a tangy, brilliant green sauce that brings a strong jolt of flavor and color to panini. Green olives, coarsely chopped and mixed with parsley, capers, garlic, and lemon zest liven up chicken breasts perfumed with sage.

Ciabatta is a thin, chewy, and very crusty flatbread that works extremely well in sandwich making; it has a minimum of crumb inside, so that the bread flavor doesn't overwhelm the taste of the filling.

2 single chicken breasts, preferably free-range

3 sprigs sage

2 garlic cloves, peeled and sliced

½ cup water

Salt and freshly ground black pepper

¾ cup chopped Italian parsley

7 green olives, pitted and coarsely chopped

2 tablespoons capers, chopped

1 small garlic clove, finely chopped

1 teaspoon chopped lemon zest

3 tablespoons extra-virgin olive oil

3 tablespoons lemon juice

2 large pieces ciabatta, each about 4 × 6 inches, or other flatbread

Arrange the chicken breast pieces side by side, skin side up, in a sauté pan just large enough to contain them. Scatter the sage and sliced garlic over the top. Add the water and season with salt and pepper. Cover tightly and cook over medium-low heat for about 15 to 20 minutes, or until the chicken is just firm to the touch. Turn off the heat and let the chicken cool in the broth.

Meanwhile, place the remaining ingredients, except the bread, in a small bowl and stir well. Add salt and pepper to taste.

When the chicken is cool enough to handle, remove the skin and bones and any fat or cartilage. Separate each chicken breast into 3 fillets. Slice on the diagonal into ½-inch-thick pieces.

Cut the ciabatta in half horizontally.

Spread three fourths of the salsa verde on the bottom halves of the bread. Arrange the sliced chicken on top of the green sauce. Then spoon the remaining sauce over the chicken. Cover with the top halves of the bread. Press down firmly so that the panino holds together, and the salsa verde soaks into the bread to flavor it.

Makes 2 panini.

37

Chicken and Peperonata on Grilled Rosemary Bread

This spicy chicken panino packs a lot of flavor and looks absolutely beautiful, with its topping of glossy red and yellow peppers and bright green basil. Adding to the rustic feeling is the dark imprint of the grill on country bread, and the scent of rosemary in the air.

If the peppers lack natural sweetness, sprinkle a little sugar over them as they cook to bring out whatever sweetness they do possess.

2 single chicken breasts, preferably free-range

½ cup water

Salt and freshly ground black pepper

4 sprigs rosemary

2 tablespoons extra-virgin olive oil

Pinch hot red pepper flakes

1 small onion, sliced

1 red and 1 yellow bell pepper, cored, seeded and cut into thick strips

Sugar to taste, optional (about 1 teaspoon)

6 oil-cured black olives, pitted and cut in half

1 tablespoon capers

8 large thin slices crusty rosemary bread

2 garlic cloves, peeled and cut in half

8 very fresh basil leaves

Place the chicken breasts skin side up in a medium sauté pan and add the water. Season the chicken with salt and pepper, and place the herb sprigs over the chicken. Cook, covered, over medium-low heat for 15 to 20 minutes, or until the flesh is just firm to the touch. Turn off the heat and let the chicken cool in the pan.

In a medium sauté pan, add the olive oil, hot red pepper flakes, and onion. Sauté over medium-low heat for about 8 minutes, stirring often. Add the peppers and continue to cook, covered, until the peppers are tender. Toward the end of the cooking, stir in the olives and capers. Season with salt and pepper to taste.

When the chicken is cool enough to handle, remove the skin and bones and any fat or cartilage. Separate each breast into 3 fillets. Cut diagonally into ½-inch-thick pieces.

Toast bread on both sides, preferably over a grill (or a stovetop cast-iron grill), or place under a hot broiler. Very lightly rub one side of each slice of bread with the cut garlic cloves.

Lay out 4 slices of the bread. Arrange the chicken on top of the bread. Top with the pepper mixture. Coarsely chop the basil and sprinkle over the peppers. Cover with the remaining 4 slices of bread.

Makes 4 big panini.

Artichoke and Tuna Panini

Artichokes and tuna have a natural affinity for each other, both densely textured and rich in flavor.

I've added a gleaming black layer of olive pesto, to give the panino a deep, tangy finish.

You can prepare your own Black Olive Pesto (see page 106) or buy imported black olive pesto.

2 6½-ounce cans imported tuna in olive oil

8–12 Marinated Baby Artichokes, homemade (see page 42)

4 crusty large round rolls

4 tablespoons Black Olive Pesto (see page 106)

½ lemon, optional

Drain the tuna. Cut the artichokes into halves or quarters lengthwise. Cut the rolls in half horizontally. If rolls are very bready, remove some of the crumb to create shallow hollows. Spread the bottom 4 halves of the rolls with black olive pesto. Top with the tuna, and then arrange the artichoke hearts over the top and drizzle with any remaining juices. Squeeze lemon juice over the artichoke hearts, if desired. Cover with the tops of the rolls. Press down on the panini to merge the ingredients.

Makes 4 panini.

40

Marinated Baby Artichokes

When I was a child, I loved marinated artichokes that come in jars. But I didn't know what love was until I tasted my first batch of homemade marinated artichokes! Start with fresh baby artichokes, boil them until tender, then marinate in good olive oil, lemon juice, and oregano. Serve in panini (see page 40) or as a savory accompaniment to panini. Baby artichokes have no choke, which makes trimming them very simple. They can be eaten after marinating an hour, or they can stay in the refrigerator for 3 or 4 days. They only get better!

1 lemon, cut in half

12 baby artichokes, about 1 pound

Salt

4 tablespoons extra-virgin olive oil

3 tablespoons lemon juice

2 teaspoons dried Mediterranean oregano, such as Greek oregano

Freshly ground black pepper

Squeeze half the lemon into a bowl of water. Reserve other half-lemon to rub into the cut portions of the artichokes to prevent darkening. Break off the tough outer leaves of the artichokes until the pale yellow leaves appear. Trim the green portion at the tips of the leaves. Trim the green surface on the base and stem of the artichokes. As you work, place each trimmed artichoke into the acidulated water.

In a nonreactive medium-sized pot, cook artichokes in salted boiling water to cover for 8 to 10 minutes, or until just tender. Drain well in a colander. Wrap in a clean dish towel to absorb water trapped between leaves.

Place the artichokes in a bowl. Add the olive oil, lemon juice, oregano, and salt and pepper to taste. Toss the artichokes in the marinade. Set aside at room temperature for an hour, stirring occasionally. Or refrigerate for up to 4 days, covered with plastic wrap.

Makes 12 marinated baby artichokes.

42

Smoked Salmon and Caprino Panini

A filling of tangy goat cheese, called caprino, is draped with delicate slice of smoked salmon. Dark green capers, flecks of sun-dried tomatoes, and a sprinkling of chives provide bright bursts of flavor and color.

2 michette, or other crusty sandwich rolls

3–4 ounces goat cheese, softened at room temperature

2 teaspoons capers

4 segments sun-dried tomatoes, cut into small pieces

2 teaspoons snipped chives

3 ounces thinly sliced smoked salmon, without preservatives or artificial color

1 tablespoon extra-virgin olive oil

1 tablespoon lemon juice

Salt and freshly ground black pepper

Small handful mixed baby lettuce leaves

Great as a filling for generous panini, the combination also works extremely well in smaller tramezzini. Cut into appetizer-size portions and serve with afternoon tea or offer with aperitifs.

Select only plump sun-dried tomatoes with tender skin and sweet flesh.

Cut the rolls in half. Spread the goat cheese on the bottom half of the rolls. Sprinkle with capers, sun-dried tomatoes, and chives. Cover with slices of smoked salmon.

In a small bowl, beat together olive oil and lemon juice. Season with salt and pepper. Spoon a little of the dressing over smoked salmon slices. Top with lettuces. Drizzle with more dressing. Cover with remaining bread.

Makes 2 panini.

43

Swordfish and Arugula Panini

Tuna in a sandwich is a long-standing tradition; fresh swordfish is something new. Here, the swordfish is grilled with a coating of fragrant green herbs. A dab of lemony mayonnaise, a sprinkling of capers, slices of juicy tomato, and leaves of bright green arugula make this a memorable panino from the sea.

For convenience, use a small stovetop grill or pan-fry the swordfish.

2 slices fresh swordfish, about ½ inch thick, each weighing 4 to 6 ounces

2 tablespoons extra-virgin olive oil

2 tablespoons mixed chopped fresh herbs including oregano, rosemary, thyme, and abundant tarragon

Salt and freshly ground black pepper

4 slices country bread

2 teaspoons Maionese al Limone (see page 52)

2 teaspoons capers

8 fresh green arugula leaves, stems trimmed

4 tomato slices

Moisten the swordfish on both sides with 1 tablespoon olive oil. Coat the grill with the remaining olive oil. Grill swordfish over gentle heat about 3 minutes on each side. Coat with herbs and season with salt and pepper. Cook for an additional 1 minute on each side, or until herbs are wilted and dark green and swordfish is tender. Transfer to a plate. Remove skin. Lightly toast the bread. Spread mayonnaise on 2 slices of bread and sprinkle with capers. Top with arugula, tomato, and swordfish. Cover with remaining bread.

Makes 2 panini.

44

Tramezzini are small panini made from *pane in cassetta*, basically the equivalent of our own white sandwich bread. Although the bread is American style, the fillings are typically Italian—creamy insalata russa, rich caponata, or delicate slices of chicken breast. It's become the fashion in Italy to eat tramezzini in the afternoon at elegant wine bars, with drinks before dinner at an outdoor *caffè*, and sometimes for a quick lunch.

The following recipes for tramezzini call for high quality white bread, either homemade or purchased from a fine bakery. Preferably it should be made from unbleached all-purpose flour and be free of any preservatives or additives.

The close-textured crumb, very fine crust, and mild flavor of *pane in cassetta* make it perfect for refined and creamy fillings. Typically, the crusts are trimmed; although this step is optional, I think it greatly enhances the tramezzini's sophisticated look.

Pane in cassetta is also used to make "toast," a panino similar to an American grilled cheese sandwich, but which contains ingredients unmistakably Italian, like fontina cheese and vegetables preserved in olive oil.

46

Avocado, Caper, and Arugula Tramezzini

Although avocado is considered rather exotic in Italy, it does appear in markets, imported from Israel and elsewhere. Avocado works beautifully here as a filling for tramezzini. The naturally creamy green flesh helps hold the tramezzino together; and the mild flavor of the bread showcases the buttery-rich flavor of the fruit.

8 slices high-quality sandwich bread (*pane in cassetta*), made from unbleached flour

1 medium avocado, ripe but firm

1 tablespoon capers

Lemon juice

Salt and freshly ground black pepper

16 small tender arugula leaves

Extra-virgin olive oil

Trim crusts from bread.

Cut the avocado in half lengthwise. Remove the pit. Cut each half again. Peel each section and cut into lengthwise slices. Fan out the avocado slices on 4 slices of bread, using ¼ of the avocado on each slice. Scatter the capers over the avocado, pressing them down lightly so they adhere. Sprinkle with lemon juice (about 1 teaspoon per tramezzino). Season with salt and pepper. Arrange the arugula leaves over the top. Season lightly with salt. Drizzle with a few drops of olive oil.

Cover with the remaining 4 slices of bread. Press down gently. Serve soon after assembling, since avocado discolors on contact with air.

Makes 4 tramezzini.

47

Black and White Tramezzino

Black olive pesto is a versatile condiment that tastes great on crostini (see page 106), tossed with pasta, or as a spread for sandwiches. Here, it gives deep, rich flavor to fresh white mozzarella.

3 ounces fresh mozzarella, packed in water

2 slices high-quality white bread (*pane in cassetta*), made from unbleached flour

2 tablespoons Black Olive Pesto (see page 106)

I love the simple, yet satisfying contrast of salty black olives and light, dairy-fresh mozzarella. This tramezzino makes a delicious lunch, along with a glass of fizzy Italian mineral water.

Slice the mozzarella and drain on tea towels. Trim the crusts off the bread (this is optional but makes the tramezzino look more "finished"). Spread pesto on both slices of bread. Layer mozzarella slices on 1 slice of bread and cover with the other bread slice.

Makes 1 tramezzino.

48

Artichoke and Tomato Tramezzini

A freshly cooked tender artichoke heart, thinly sliced, layered with rounds of juicy tomato, and enriched with lemony mayonnaise, makes a light, elegant tramezzino filling.

1 medium artichoke

½ lemon

Salt

1 tablespoon lemon juice

1 tablespoon extra-virgin olive oil

Freshly ground black pepper

2 teaspoons Maionese al Limone (see page 52)

4 slices white sandwich bread (*pane in cassetta*), made from unbleached flour

1 crisp medium-sized tomato, sliced

Select an artichoke with tightly clenched leaves, a sign of freshness. An artichoke heavy for its size will provide a large edible base.

To prevent artichoke from darkening, use the lemon half to rub the cut portions of the artichoke while you work. Snap back and pull off the dark green leaves of the artichoke, working your way around the base. Stop when you get to the tender, pale yellow leaves. With a paring knife, trim away dark green areas around the base of the artichoke. Cut across the top of the artichoke, leaving about ½ inch of tender leaves. Trim the stalk, leaving about 1 inch. Cut deeply to trim away the dark green fibers around the outside of the stalk. Cut the artichoke in half lengthwise.

Place the artichoke halves, cut side down, in a nonreactive saucepan just large enough to contain them. Add water measuring 1 inch up the side of the pan. Add salt. Cook over medium heat, tightly covered, until the artichoke is just tender. Drain, and when cool enough to handle, pull away the choke. If necessary, use a paring knife to trim away any remaining choke. Thinly slice the artichoke. Place in a bowl with the olive oil and lemon juice, and season with salt and pepper to taste.

While the artichoke marinates, make the mayonnaise.

Trim the crusts from the bread. This is optional, but the tramezzini will look more "finished."

Spread mayonnaise on 2 slices of bread. Layer with the artichoke slices and top with tomato slices. Season the tomato with salt. Cover with the remaining 2 slices of bread.

Makes 2 tramezzini.

50

Maionese al Limone

This pastel yellow, light-textured mayonnaise is made with 1 whole egg rather than all egg yolks. The tart, tingly flavor and sweet perfume of lemon make it an ideal spread for all kinds of panini that are enhanced by a bit of richness.

1 egg, preferably cage-free, at room temperature

¼ teaspoon salt

¾ cup olive oil

Juice of ½ lemon

For variety, add finely snipped chives, chopped tarragon, crushed anchovies, lemon zest, or capers. For a lovely green-tinted mayonnaise, process fresh basil leaves in a blender or food processor with a little olive oil and stir into the mayonnaise.

Lemon mayonnaise lasts for several days. Just wrap tightly and store in the refrigerator.

Combine the egg, salt, and 3 tablespoons olive oil in a blender. Blend until the mixture is light yellow. With blender running, add the remaining olive oil in a slow, steady, thin stream. Stop pouring only if the oil is not being absorbed. Blend without adding any more oil until the oil in the blender is absorbed. Continue adding the remaining oil in a thin stream. Add the lemon juice and blend briefly. Adjust the seasonings, adding more salt or lemon juice if needed. Transfer to a small bowl. Cover tightly and refrigerate until needed.

Makes 1 cup.

Note: The United States Department of Agriculture has issued a warning about the use of raw eggs. If you feel you may be at risk, do not make dishes which feature raw eggs, including mayonnaise.

52

Tuna and Black Olive Butter Tramezzini

I first tasted this spread one summer in Italy at a party at the beach house of relatives who live in Rome.

Everyone pitched in to prepare a simple dinner eaten on the terrace: spaghettini with sun-dried tomatoes and arugula, spicy stuffed eggs, platters of prosciutto and cheeses, and a tuna spread, playfully formed into the shape of a fish!

The tuna spread, enriched with Black Olive Pesto (see page 106) and dotted with capers, makes an easy, flavorful filling for tramezzini.

A side note: Canned tuna, always packed in olive oil, is used often in Italy. It is a long-standing custom to preserve it in oil, since at one time fresh tuna was only available seasonally.

6½ ounces imported canned tuna in olive oil, drained

4 tablespoons unsalted butter, softened at room temperature

3 small anchovies, chopped

2 teaspoons Black Olive Pesto (see page 106)

1 tablespoon capers

12 slices high-quality white bread (*pane in cassetta*), made from unbleached flour

Place tuna, butter, and anchovies in a blender or food processor and blend until mixture is smooth and fluffy. Transfer spread to a small bowl. Stir in the black olive pesto and capers.

Trim the crusts from the bread.

Spread the mixture on half the bread slices, stopping short of the edges by about ½ inch. Cover with the remaining bread slices. If desired, cut the tramezzini in squares or triangles, and serve with before-dinner drinks.

Makes 6 tramezzini or 24 appetizers.

53

Insalata Russa and Shrimp Tramezzini

The filling for these elegant tramezzini is a creamy mixture of shrimp and finely diced vegetables bound with homemade Maionese al Limone (see page 52). The vegetables must be cut into small, neat dice; this helps the insalata russa hold together and creates a careful and polished-looking filling. Cook the vegetables until tender but firm; crunchy vegetables are out of place in insalata russa.

Serve with cold white wine for a clean, crisp counterpoint to the richness of the mayonnaise.

2 small carrots, peeled and trimmed

Salt

¼ pound tender green beans, ends trimmed

2–3 small potatoes of equal size, about ¼ pound

½ pound medium raw shrimp

2 tablespoons capers

2 tablespoons chopped cornichons

1 tablespoon extra-virgin olive oil

1 tablespoon lemon juice

Freshly ground black pepper

4–6 tablespoons Maionese al Limone (see page 52)

12 slices white bread (*pane in cassetta*), made from unbleached flour

Cut the carrots into thirds. Cook in salted boiling water until tender but firm. Drain well and let cool. Cut into small dice.

Cook the green beans in salted boiling water until tender but firm. Drain well and let cool. Gather the green beans lengthwise in a bundle and cut across into very small pieces.

Boil the potatoes in salted water until tender. Drain well and when cool enough to handle, peel them. Let potatoes cool completely, then cut into small dice. If you try to dice them when warm, the potatoes will fall apart. Devein the shrimp by making a shallow cut lengthwise on the outside curve of the shell, cutting right through the shell. Discard any black vein. Rinse the shrimp under cool running water. Cook the shrimp in salted boiling water very briefly, 1 to 2 minutes, until they turn pink and the flesh is just opaque. Drain well. When cool, use a very sharp knife to cut shrimp into neat dice.

Combine shrimp and all the prepared ingredients in a bowl. Add the capers and cornichons, and stir gently. Season with olive oil, lemon juice, and salt and pepper to taste. Set aside while you prepare the mayonnaise. (For convenience, the mayonnaise may be made in advance.)

Gently fold mayonnaise into the salad, just enough to bind the salad. Add more mayonnaise for a richer insalata russa that holds together a little better. Correct seasonings.

Continued

Continued from page 54

Trim the crusts from the bread. This is optional but makes the tramezzini look more "finished." Spoon the salad on half the bread slices and spread evenly, stopping short about ½ inch from the edge. Top with the remaining bread slices, pressing down gently to bind the filling to the bread. To serve as appetizers, cut tramezzini into quarters.

Makes 6 tramezzini or 24 appetizers.

Whole Grain Tramezzini with Smoked Salmon

Smoked salmon, cucumber, and watercress in an Italian sandwich? Yes, when the bread is thinly sliced *pane integrale*, Italian whole grain bread, and the panino is moistened with fruity olive oil and fragrant lemon juice.

56

1 small handful watercress sprigs, coarse stems removed

1 tablespoon extra-virgin olive oil

1 teaspoon lemon juice

Salt and freshly ground black pepper

4 thin slices whole grain bread (*pane integrale*)

Extra-virgin olive oil

Fresh lemon juice

3 ounces thinly sliced smoked salmon, without coloring or preservatives

Slightly less than ¼ seedless cucumber, peeled and thinly sliced

No sliced whole wheat bread from the supermarket here. The bread must have a coarse texture and a warm, toasty flavor. Slice it thinly so that the bread flavor doesn't overwhelm the other ingredients. The result—a sophisticated tramezzino, delightful with afternoon tea.

Toss the watercress with the 1 tablespoon olive oil and 1 teaspoon lemon juice. Season with salt and pepper to taste.

Trim the crusts from the bread. This is optional but makes the tramezzini look more "finished."

Drizzle 2 of the bread slices very lightly with more olive oil and lemon juice. Arrange the smoked salmon on top. Cover with cucumber slices. Season lightly with salt and pepper. Top with the watercress salad and cover with the other slices of bread.

Makes 2 tramezzini.

Chicken Tramezzini with Lemon Butter

Pine nuts and currants stud this extraordinary chicken tramezzino, sprinkled with slivers of russet-red radicchio. *Pane in cassetta* is spread with butter, flavored with lemon zest and lemon juice to enrich and perfume the filling.

2 small chicken breasts, preferably free-range

½ cup water

3 sprigs rosemary

2 garlic cloves, peeled and sliced

Salt

3 tablespoons unsalted butter, softened at room temperature

Zest of ½ lemon, preferably organic

1 tablespoon lemon juice

8 slices white bread (*pane in cassetta*), made from unbleached flour

1 tablespoon lightly toasted pine nuts

1 tablespoon plumped currants

4 large tender radicchio leaves, cut into strips

When using lemon zest or rind in cooking, seek out organic fruit in order to avoid high concentrations of pesticides.

Place the chicken breasts, skin side up, in a sauté pan just large enough to contain them. Add water, rosemary, garlic, and salt to taste. Cover and cook over medium heat for about 15 minutes, or until the chicken is just firm to the touch. Let cool in its juices.

Meanwhile, in a small bowl combine the butter, lemon zest, lemon juice, and salt to taste. Mix with a fork until well blended. Set aside until needed. When the chicken is cool, lift out of the pan. Remove skin, bones, and any fat or cartilage. Divide meat into large fillets. Cut fillets crosswise into diagonal slices about ¼ inch thick.

Lightly butter all 8 slices of bread. Trim the crusts. Sprinkle 4 slices of bread with pine nuts and currants. Arrange chicken slices on top. Sprinkle strips of radicchio over the chicken. Cover with the remaining bread slices and press down gently on each tramezzino with the palm of your hand so it holds together.

Makes 4 tramezzini.

57

Fontina "Toast"

A "toast" is the Italian version of a grilled cheese sandwich. Besides cheese, there might be some prosciutto, marinated mushrooms, roasted peppers, or artichokes. In this version, thin slices of fontina are topped with marinated red peppers and mushrooms, then the "toast" is grilled until the cheese melts.

Purchase high-quality marinated vegetables, or make your own. See pages 60, 30, and 42 for simple recipes for marinated mushrooms, red peppers, and artichokes.

3–4 ounces imported Italian fontina, thinly sliced and cut to fit the bread

4 slices white bread (pane in cassetta), made from unbleached flour

8 thin strips of marinated red peppers

8 marinated mushrooms, sliced

Salt and freshly ground black pepper

Arrange the fontina on 2 slices of bread. Arrange peppers and mushrooms over the cheese. Cover with the remaining 2 slices of bread.

Place the "toasts" on a hot, lightly oiled stovetop grill and weigh down with a heavy pan. Cook, turning once, until the cheese melts and both sides of the bread are golden brown and marked by the grill. Alternately, use a sandwich grill and cook until the cheese melts and the bread is golden. Serve hot.

Makes 2 "toasts."

58

Marinated Mushrooms

Marinated mushrooms are a breeze to make and taste much better than store-bought.

You can spice the marinade with a pinch of hot red pepper flakes and some balsamic vinegar and scent it with just about any herb growing in the garden. The mushrooms are ready to eat when they have soaked up enough marinade to flavor them fully; an hour is sufficient, but overnight is best. Sliced marinated mushrooms add texture and tang to all sorts of sandwich fillings; or mound them in rolls lined with tender lettuce leaves for mushroom panini. A few perched next to a panino make an attractive accompaniment—juicy little morsels to savor between bites.

1 pound button mushrooms, all about the same size if possible

6 tablespoons extra-virgin olive oil

Juice of 1 lemon, about ¼ cup

⅓ cup water

2 large garlic cloves, peeled and cut into thick slices

4 fresh thyme sprigs

2 fresh sage leaves

1 bay leaf

Small pinch hot red pepper flakes, about ⅛ teaspoon

A few black peppercorns

1 teaspoon salt

2 tablespoons balsamic vinegar, optional

Wipe the mushrooms clean with damp paper towels. Trim stems if necessary. Cut any very large mushrooms in half.

Heat 3 tablespoons olive oil in a large sauté pan. Add mushrooms and sauté over low heat until just tender. Transfer to a bowl.

Place remaining olive oil, lemon, water, garlic, herbs, hot red pepper flakes, black peppercorns, and salt in sauté pan. Simmer for 5 minutes. Pour over the mushrooms in the bowl. Stir in the optional balsamic vinegar. Let mushrooms cool in marinade. Cover and refrigerate overnight. Bring to room temperature before serving. To serve, lift out of marinade with a slotted spoon.

Makes 2 cups marinated mushrooms.

60

4-Seasons Pizza Romana

Pizza Romana, a Roman specialty, is made with flat focaccia bread filled with mozzarella and tomatoes or prosciutto, then grilled until the cheese melts. Whenever I'm in Rome I stop at Bar Vanni, famous for its terrific panini, to order it. At home, one bite conjures up Rome on a hot summer night, crowds in the street, bright lights in the bar, and the smell of espresso and grilled bread in the air. This version of Pizza Romana is inspired by one of my favorite pizzas.

8 medium mushrooms

2 teaspoons extra-virgin olive oil

Salt

4 ounces fresh mozzarella, packed in water

6 Marinated Baby Artichokes (see page 42)

4 large thin slices imported prosciutto

6 oil-cured black olives

4 squares or rounds of focaccia

1 red ripe Roma tomato, cored, seeded, and diced

Extra-virgin olive oil for drizzling

Freshly ground black pepper

Dried Mediterranean oregano, such as Greek oregano

Wipe the mushrooms clean with damp paper towels. Trim the stems and thickly slice the mushrooms. Place olive oil in a small sauté pan. Turn heat to high and add mushrooms. Sauté until golden around the edges. Lightly salt mushrooms and set aside.

Drain the mozzarella. Thinly slice the cheese and spread out on a folded tea towel to drain again. Slice the artichokes. Cut the prosciutto in half crosswise. Pit and coarsely chop the olives.

Slice the focaccia in half horizontally. Drizzle the insides of the bread very lightly with olive oil. Keep all ingredients about ½ inch from the edges of the bread. Arrange 2 slices of prosciutto on the bottom halves of the bread. Distribute the mozzarella over the prosciutto. Top with tomato, artichokes, mushrooms, and olives. Season lightly with salt and pepper and sprinkle with a small pinch of oregano. Cover with the top halves of the bread and press down firmly.

Place focaccia panini either on a stovetop grill or in a skillet and weigh down with a heavy pan. Grill panini over medium-high heat, turning them once. They are ready when the cheese melts, about 5 to 6 minutes. Serve immediately.

Makes 4 panini.

61

Rosemary Focaccia with Ricotta and Swiss Chard

Ricotta, sun-dried tomatoes, and Swiss chard, spiked with hot red pepper are layered in rosemary focaccia. Serve the panino warm and fragrant from the oven. Young Swiss chard has succulent white stems and green leaves. Supermarket chard often has stems and leaves that appear to have been waging some kind of battle—all torn and tattered and bruised. Farmer's markets and natural foods stores are the best sources for Swiss chard. And nothing rivals garden-fresh chard.

1 bunch Swiss chard, about ¾ pound

Salt

2 tablespoons extra-virgin olive oil plus extra for drizzling

1 large garlic clove, peeled and finely chopped

Pinch hot red pepper flakes

¾ pound ricotta, well drained in several layers of cheesecloth

3–4 moist sun-dried tomatoes, cut into small pieces

3 tablespoons freshly grated imported Parmesan cheese

Freshly ground black pepper

4 squares rosemary focaccia

Trim the stems of the Swiss chard. Strip the leaves from the stems. Coarsely chop leaves. Cut stems into small dice.

Place about ½ cup of water in a medium sauté pan. Add the diced Swiss chard and place the leaves on top. Sprinkle with a little salt. Cover and cook over medium heat for about 4 or 5 minutes, or until tender. Stir once or twice while cooking. Check to make sure the water does not completely evaporate, and, if necessary, add a little more water. Swiss chard with thicker stalks will require a longer cooking time. Drain chard well in a colander and gently press out excess water with the back of a wooden spoon.

Place olive oil, garlic, and hot red pepper flakes in a medium sauté pan. Cook over low heat for about 2 to 3 minutes. Add Swiss chard and toss. Cook over medium-low heat for about 5 minutes, stirring occasionally, until excess moisture evaporates.

Place the ricotta, sun-dried tomatoes, and Parmesan in a small bowl. Season with salt and pepper to taste.

Meanwhile, split the focaccia in half horizontally. Grill focaccia halves cut side down, or toast them, cut side up, under the broiler. Drizzle cut sides lightly with olive oil. Place a layer of ricotta mixture on the bottom half of the bread. Top with chard. Cover with the other half of the bread. Place in a 450° oven until bread is hot and crusty. Serve warm.

Makes 4 panini.

62

Focaccia with Sautéed Mushrooms

Focaccia, a type of flatbread, makes wonderful panini. It doesn't have a lot of crumb to compete with the filling, and the crust crisps up nicely in the oven.

The following recipe is especially good when made with herb focaccia, since the bread echoes the strong herbal flavors in the mushroom filling; but unflavored focaccia works just as well.

If you can find them, use cremini mushrooms and a few meaty shiitakes. Button mushrooms can be used, too. Shiitake mushrooms must be added toward the end of the cooking, since they lose their texture rather quickly and become unappealingly slippery.

1 ounce dried porcini mushrooms

1 tablespoon extra-virgin olive oil

1 small onion, finely diced

1 tablespoon unsalted butter

2 tablespoons extra-virgin olive oil

1 pound assorted fresh mushrooms, wiped clean, trimmed, and thickly sliced

1 teaspoon chopped rosemary

1 teaspoon chopped thyme

3 tablespoons chopped Italian parsley

2 large garlic cloves, peeled and minced

Salt and freshly ground black pepper

4 rounds or squares of focaccia

Extra-virgin olive oil for drizzling

Rinse porcini under cold running water. Soak them in a small bowl in hot water for about 20 minutes. Lift the mushrooms out of the soaking liquid. Strain liquid and reserve for use in soups and stews. Cut porcini into thick strips.

Meanwhile place 1 tablespoon olive oil in a small sauté pan. Add the onion and sauté over low heat for 15 minutes, or until tender and soft. If onions start to stick, add a little water to the pan, a few tablespoons at a time. Place the butter and 2 tablespoons olive oil in a large sauté pan. Turn heat to high. Add the fresh mushrooms and cook, stirring only occasionally to allow the mushrooms to brown and become crusty around the edges. When all excess moisture evaporates and the mushrooms are nicely browned, lower the heat and add the onion, porcini, herbs, garlic, and salt and pepper to taste. Stir well.

Meanwhile split the focaccia horizontally. Place, cut side up, under a hot broiler until the insides are lightly toasted. Remove focaccia from oven and drizzle toasted sides very lightly with olive oil. Divide warm mushroom mixture among the 4 bottom halves. Cover with the top halves. Place focaccia panini in a 450° oven until the focaccia are hot and crusty.

Makes 4 panini.

Herb Frittata Panino

The first person who thought of putting a frittata between slices of bread deserves a prize. A frittata panino makes a light, nourishing lunch that can be prepared in a flash with ingredients most people have on hand.

Here, a fragrant herb frittata is the filling for this easy panino. The recipe calls for a mix of marjoram, basil, and chives—but just about any fresh herbs can be used.

2 eggs, preferably cage-free

1 tablespoon chopped basil

1 tablespoon snipped chives

1 teaspoon chopped marjoram

1 small garlic clove, peeled and very finely chopped

1 tablespoon freshly grated imported Parmesan cheese

Salt and freshly ground black pepper

1 tablespoon unsalted butter

2–4 slices country bread

Crack the eggs into a bowl and beat lightly with a fork. Add the herbs, garlic, Parmesan, and salt and pepper to taste. Mix well.

Place the butter in a small, nonstick ovenproof sauté pan. Turn the heat to high and when the butter just begins to brown, add the egg mixture. Turn down the heat and stir the eggs until curds form. Let the frittata cook until the bottom is firm but the top is still runny. Place the sauté pan under a hot broiler and cook until the top is just firm.

Unmold the frittata onto a plate. Serve the frittata warm or at room temperature. If desired, lightly toast the bread. To make 1 panino, fold the frittata in half and place between 2 slices of bread. To make 2 panini, cut the frittata in half and place each half between bread slices.

Makes 1 to 2 panini.

65

Spinach Frittata Panini

Nestled into a split roll, a lovely green and gold spinach frittata becomes a delicious treat to tuck into a lunchbox or take along on a picnic.

If cage-free eggs are available in your area, I urge you to try them. They have superior flavor and color—the yolks are bright orange, not the anemic color of supermarket eggs.

1 small bunch tender green spinach

Salt

1 tablespoon extra-virgin olive oil

1 garlic clove, peeled and finely minced

3 eggs, preferably cage-free

2 tablespoons grated Pecorino Romano cheese

1 tablespoon unsalted butter

1 tablespoon extra-virgin olive oil

2 large baguette-shaped rolls

Unsalted butter, softened at room temperature, to spread on rolls

Trim the stalks from the spinach. Wash the spinach leaves by placing in a large bowl or sink full of cold water. Change the water about 3 times, or until the bottom of the bowl or sink is completely free of grit.

Lift the spinach out of the water and place in a sauté pan with just the water that clings to the leaves. Sprinkle with salt. Cover and cook over high heat. After a minute or two, remove the cover and stir. Lower the heat to medium and continue to cook until the spinach is just barely wilted. Drain well in a colander. Use the back of a wooden spoon to gently press out excess moisture. Coarsely chop the spinach.

Place 1 tablespoon olive oil and the garlic in a small, ovenproof sauté pan measuring about 6 inches in diameter. Cook over low heat for a minute or two, then add the spinach. Toss spinach, adding salt to taste. Stir over medium heat until any remaining moisture in the spinach evaporates, about 1 to 2 minutes. Let cool.

Break the eggs into a bowl and beat with a fork. Add grated cheese and cooled spinach and mix well.

Wipe the sauté pan clean with a paper towel. Add 1 tablespoon butter and 1 tablespoon olive oil to the pan. Turn the heat to high and stir. When the foam begins to subside, add the egg mixture all at once. Use a wooden spoon to pull egg mixture away from sides of pan toward the center, until large curds form. When the bottom of the frittata begins to firm up, place the pan under a hot broiler and cook until the frittata is just firm all the way through. Unmold onto a plate and let cool.

Split the rolls in half lengthwise. Very lightly butter both sides of the rolls. Cut the frittata in half and place on the bottom halves of the rolls. Cover with the tops of the rolls.

Makes 2 panini.

66

Golden Polenta Panini

If you love polenta as much as I do, you will want to try these little panini in which rounds of polenta take the place of bread. The filling? A tasty combination of fontina and prosciutto. The panini are fried until the polenta is crisp and golden on the outside and the cheese has melted to a fragrant cream.

1 recipe Fast Polenta (see page 68)

8 ounces imported Italian fontina, cut into 12 thin rounds, each a little smaller than the polenta rounds

4 ounces imported Italian prosciutto, cut into 24 pieces, each about the same size as the cheese rounds

Salt and freshly ground black pepper

3 eggs, preferably cage-free

¾ cup unbleached flour

½ cup bread crumbs

Olive oil for frying

Prepare polenta according to directions on page 68. With a wet spatula, spread hot polenta on a lightly oiled 10½ × 15½-inch cookie sheet to a ½-inch thickness and smooth top. Let cool. Use a cookie cutter or glass to form 24 rounds about 2 inches in diameter. Polenta trimmings can be sprinkled with Parmesan cheese and butter, and baked in the oven.

Place a round of fontina and 2 pieces of prosciutto over half of the polenta rounds. Season with a little salt and pepper to taste. Top with the remaining polenta rounds.

Crack the eggs into a bowl and beat well, adding a little salt. Spread the flour on a dinner plate and the bread crumbs on another dinner plate.

In a large, heavy sauté pan, add oil to measure ¼ inch up the sides. Heat oil until hot but not smoking. Roll the edges of the panini through the flour, then dip edges in egg, and roll in bread crumbs. Bread and fry only a few panini at a time.

Cook the polenta panini in the oil on both sides until crisp. Using tongs, lift the panini one by one and fry the edges until golden brown (this seals in the melting cheese). If the exterior of the polenta is turning golden brown but the cheese is not completely melted, turn down the heat.

Use tongs to remove the panini from the pan, letting excess oil drain back into the pan. Drain panini well on several layers of paper towels. Sprinkle lightly with salt. Serve immediately on dishes lined with white paper napkins to absorb any remaining oil.

Makes 12 small panini.

67

Fast Polenta

When polenta undergoes a second cooking, such as grilling or frying, instant polenta is a great fast alternative to traditional methods. Use for all recipes in the book that call for polenta.

6½ cups water

2 teaspoons salt

1 13-ounce box (2 cups) instant polenta

Bring the water to a boil and add salt. Quickly add the polenta in steady stream, stirring continously with a wooden spoon. Reduce heat to medium and continue stirring for 5 minutes, or until the polenta is thick, soft, and smooth.

Pour polenta into a moistened 1½-quart loaf pan or onto a lightly oiled 10½ × 15½-inch baking sheet. Smooth the top with a wet spatula. Let cool. If making ahead, cover with plastic wrap and refrigerate for up to 24 hours.

Proceed as directed in recipes calling for polenta.

Makes enough polenta to fill a 1 ½-quart loaf pan or a 10½ × 15½-inch cookie sheet.

Panini Fritti

I adore fried eggplant. Yes, fried! When the eggplant slices hit the hot oil they transform from pale and mild to burnished gold and deeply flavored.

Here, eggplant takes the place of bread. As the panino fries, the flesh of the eggplant and the smoked mozzarella become a savory cream encased by the golden exterior.

Very southern Italian in spirit, it's easy to imagine eating these at a bustling *caffè* in Naples. Serve on individual plates lined with white paper napkins, to absorb any remaining oil. That's how it's done in Italy!

1 firm medium eggplant

½ pound fresh, moist smoked mozzarella

2 tablespoons chopped basil leaves

1 teaspoon dried Mediterranean oregano, such as Greek oregano

Salt and freshly ground black pepper

½ cup unbleached flour

3 eggs, preferably cage-free

1 cup unflavored bread crumbs

Olive oil for frying

Trim stem end of eggplant. Slice eggplant horizontally into rounds ¼ inch thick to make 16 slices of eggplant. If time permits, salt eggplant slices and let drain for 1 hour, drain off excess water, and wipe dry.

Slice the mozzarella thinly.

To assemble panini, select pairs of eggplant slices of similar size. Arrange the mozzarella on half the eggplant slices, leaving a ½-inch border of eggplant. Sprinkle with basil and oregano. Season with salt and pepper to taste. Cover with the remaining eggplant slices. Press down firmly to bind ingredients.

Spread flour on a dinner plate. Break eggs into a shallow soup bowl. Beat eggs well and season with a little salt. Spread bread crumbs on another dinner plate. Holding 2 slices of eggplant together, carefully flour both sides of the panino. Dip the panino into the eggs, letting excess drain off. Then dip in the bread crumbs and gently shake off excess. Make sure to coat the sides of the panino as well as the flat surfaces.

In a large, heavy sauté pan, add enough oil to measure ¼ inch up the side of the pan. When the oil is hot, but not smoking, carefully place a few eggplant panini in the hot oil and fry on both sides until golden brown. Do not crowd the pan. Bread and fry only 2 or 3 panini at a time. Adjust heat as necessary to keep the cooking lively, but do not allow oil to smoke. If the oil level goes down, add more oil as needed, but not while panini are cooking; add oil between batches.

Drain the panini on several layers of paper towels and salt lightly. Serve piping hot.

Makes 8 small panini.

71

Bruschetta: The Original Garlic Bread

Bruschetta is the original garlic bread. In its authentic form, it bears little relationship to garlic bread as it is known in America. Although they both contain the same basic ingredients—bread and garlic—the similarities end there.

Bruschetta begins with a thick slice of country bread. The bread is grilled over fragrant coals, then rubbed with a cut clove of garlic. Next comes a drizzle of rich and fruity olive oil, a sprinkling of sea salt, and perhaps some fresh black pepper. Although grilling the bread is the time-honored method, bruschetta can also be made under the broiler or even popped in the toaster. The idea is to turn the surface of the bread golden and crisp, rough enough to break down the garlic, with enough heat from the bread to release the fragrance of the garlic and olive oil.

The appeal of bruschetta is basic and earthy—the robust pleasure of biting into coarse country bread, the warm perfume of fresh garlic, the sensuous delight of luminous green olive oil. The demands placed on the cook are few; bruschetta is indeed one of the simplest dishes in the Italian repertoire.

Its very simplicity lends itself to countless variations. After the ritual of grilling the bread, rubbing it with garlic, and moistening it with olive oil, the bread can be sprinkled with herbs or made more substantial with a variety of toppings. The classic bruschetta topping—the one most often used in country kitchens and trattorias across Italy—is simply brilliant red chopped tomatoes scattered with torn basil leaves.

Most often served as an antipasto or first course, bruschetta can easily be transformed into a quick lunch dish: mound bruschetta with ricotta and accompany with black olives for an easy, nutritious, and satisfying midday meal for one. As

73

the main offering of a rustic dinner, bruschetta can be the base for crushed fava beans and sautéed greens, served with a salad and red wine. Bruschetta is adaptable to less traditionally Italian ingredients: Unorthodox but delicious is a topping of avocado and capers. For a very special occasion, serve bruschetta with paper-thin slices of black or white truffles on top. The permutations are infinite, but the key is to keep it simple.

Bruschetta knows no season: In summer use tomatoes just picked from the garden, still warm and spicy-smelling; in winter make a coarse puree of broccoli and black olives; in spring top the bruschetta with tender leaves of arugula. Just fire up the grill, heat up the broiler, or plug in your toaster. That's all it takes. With very little effort, you can create one of the great rustic dishes of Italy.

74

Bruschetta

Traditionally bruschetta was eaten in the olive-producing regions of Italy during the winter, when olives, ripened to a purple hue, but not yet black, are pressed for their oil. The first pressing—deep green, dense, unfiltered—was drizzled generously over thick slices of country bread grilled over wood coals.

Originally a rural dish, bruschetta has become fashionable all over Italy. It's become wildly popular in America, too, and deservedly so.

This bruschetta should ideally be eaten as a separate course, preceding the meal, so that it can be fully savored.

4 slices crusty, firm-crumbed country bread, cut about ¾ inch thick

2 large fresh garlic cloves, peeled and cut in half

Very fruity, rich-tasting extra-virgin olive oil

Sea salt

Coarsely ground black pepper, optional

Grill or toast the bread on both sides until golden brown, but not hard-toasted all the way through. Rub one side of each slice of bread with the cut garlic cloves. The garlic will break down and become absorbed into the bread. The more you rub, the more pungent the garlic flavor. Place the bread on a serving dish with the garlic-rubbed side up. Drizzle generously with olive oil. Season with salt to taste, and pepper if desired. Serve immediately.

Makes 4 bruschettas.

75

Bruschetta al Salmoriglio

This simple bruschetta takes grilled bread one step further—a dressing of olive oil, lemon juice, and dried oregano, called salmoriglio, is brushed over the hot bread to release an explosion of aromatic, sultry scents. If possible, buy branches of dried oregano and coarsely crumble the leaves and flowers.

Delicious at the beginning of a meal, Bruschetta al Salmoriglio also makes an extraordinary accompaniment for grilled seafood and seafood soups.

4 slices country bread, preferably Sicilian, cut ½ inch thick

3 tablespoons extra-virgin olive oil

2 tablespoons lemon juice

2 teaspoons dried Mediterranean oregano, such as Greek oregano

Very small pinch hot red pepper flakes

Sea salt and coarsely ground black pepper to taste

2 garlic cloves, peeled and cut in half

Grill or toast the bread.

Meanwhile, combine in a small bowl the olive oil, lemon juice, oregano, hot red pepper flakes, and salt and pepper to taste. Beat with a fork until creamy.

When the bread is golden on both sides and marked by the grill, rub cut garlic lightly into one side of each slice of bread. Generously brush with dressing. Allow dressing to soak into the bread, then brush on a little more.

Makes 4 bruschettas.

Bruschetta al Prosciutto

I've loved prosciutto ever since I was a child. It was always part of the buffet my parents offered when their Italian friends gathered at our house for a party.

What could be more natural than pink, buttery slices of prosciutto draped over grilled country bread? If possible, use Parma prosciutto, sliced a little thicker than paper-thin. If sliced too thin, the prosciutto becomes extremely fragile, tears easily, and the full flavor can't be appreciated.

When figs are in season, in June and in the fall, serve the bruschetta surrounded by ripe figs.

Ideal for brunch, as a light lunch, as a first course, or anytime in between!

4 slices country bread, cut ½ to ¾ inch thick

2 garlic cloves, peeled and cut in half

Extra-virgin olive oil

4 slices imported Italian prosciutto, about ⅙ pound

8–12 figs, stemmed and cut in half lengthwise

Grill the bread on both sides until crusty on the outside but still soft within. Rub one side of each slice of bread with cut garlic. Arrange bread slices on a platter and drizzle with a little olive oil. Top each slice of bread with a slice of prosciutto and surround with figs.

Makes 4 bruschettas.

Bruschetta with Arugula Salad

In Italy, wild arugula is gathered in the countryside and sold in the outdoor markets that are the heartbeat of every town and city. Whether wild or cultivated, arugula's beautifully shaped leaf has a pronounced oaky, peppery flavor. In this recipe, the leaves are tossed with olive oil and lemon juice to become a topping for garlic-rubbed grilled bread.

If arugula is unavailable, watercress makes an excellent substitute. Although it lacks arugula's unique flavor, watercress also packs a peppery punch, has a tender leaf, and possesses the strong green coloring that indicates its powerful health-enhancing properties.

4 slices country bread, cut about ¾ inch thick

2 garlic cloves, peeled and cut in half

Extra-virgin olive oil for drizzling on bread

2–3 small bunches bright green arugula, stems trimmed

1 tablespoon extra-virgin olive oil

1 tablespoon lemon juice

Sea salt

Grill or toast the bread on both sides until golden. Rub the bread on one side with the cut garlic and drizzle lightly with olive oil.

Quickly toss the arugula with 1 tablespoon olive oil, the lemon juice, and salt to taste. Taste and add more oil and lemon juice if necessary. Mound arugula on each slice of bread.

Makes 4 bruschettas.

80

Bruschetta all'Avocado

The scent of fresh green avocado mashed with lemon juice reminds me of my childhood in southern California. My best friend lived in the heart of a shady avocado grove, and all season long I would receive a steady supply. My mother used to fix avocados for me as an afternoon snack, mashed with lemon juice and salt and spread on French bread.

Here, I've taken my snack and given it an Italian twist by spreading the coarse puree on bruschetta and by sprinkling capers and oregano on top.

Select an avocado that is firm but yields to gentle pressure; overripe or bruised avocados have an unpleasantly flat taste.

1 medium avocado

2 tablespoons lemon juice

Salt

4 slices country bread, cut about ¾ inch thick

1 large garlic clove, peeled and cut in half

Extra-virgin olive oil

1 teaspoon dried Mediterranean oregano, such as Greek oregano

1 tablespoon capers

Peel and pit the avocado and mash it with the lemon juice and salt to taste. Toast the bread until golden brown. Rub one side of the bread with the cut garlic clove and drizzle very lightly with a few drops of olive oil.

Spread the avocado on the bread and top with a sprinkling of oregano and capers.

Makes 4 bruschettas.

81

Bruschetta with Ammogghiu Sauce

Ammogghiu, a popular Sicilian sauce for grilled fish, does double duty as a topping for bruschetta.

Naturally the tastier the tomatoes, the better the sauce. In Sicily, tomatoes grow in a nearly arid climate, yet are incredibly sweet, juicy, and full of flesh. Slather the sauce on thick slices of grilled Sicilian bread for a true taste of Sicily.

1 pound red ripe tomatoes

2 medium-sized fresh white garlic cloves, peeled

¾ cup very fragrant basil leaves

Small pinch hot red pepper flakes

Sea salt

3 tablespoons extra-virgin olive oil

6 thick slices Sicilian bread or other country bread

Plunge the tomatoes in boiling water to cover for about 10 seconds, or roast them very briefly over a grill or gas flame until just slightly charred. Peel and seed the tomatoes, and squeeze out excess water. Chop the tomatoes to a coarse puree and place in a bowl.

Place on a chopping board the garlic, basil, hot red pepper flakes, and a generous pinch of salt. Finely chop the ingredients, using the flat side of the blade to make a rough pesto. Alternatively, you can use a mortar and pestle. In both methods the salt helps break down the ingredients into a pesto.

If using a chopping block, transfer the ingredients to a small bowl and beat in about 3 tablespoons of olive oil, or enough to create a loose pesto sauce. If using a mortar and pestle, add the olive oil to the ingredients in the mortar.

Add the pesto to the tomatoes and stir well. Taste and correct seasonings, adding more salt or red pepper flakes as needed. The sauce can be used immediately or left to rest at room temperature for 1 to 2 hours to develop the flavors.

Grill the bread on both sides until grill marks appear and the bread is golden and well toasted throughout. Stir the sauce well and spoon it over the bread slices. Serve immediately.

Makes 6 bruschettas.

Bruschetta alla Bella Napoli

Here's a bruschetta that is easy to make and that everyone loves. The bruschetta is briefly popped in the oven until the smoked mozzarella melts and is barely flecked with gold, then topped with a spoonful of finely diced raw tomato seasoned with fragrant garlic and oregano.

1 ripe but firm medium tomato, cored and finely diced

1 teaspoon dried Mediterranean oregano, such as Greek oregano

1 teaspoon extra-virgin olive oil

Salt

4 slices country bread, about ¾ inch thick

Extra-virgin olive oil

¼ pound smoked mozzarella, shredded

In a small bowl combine the tomato, oregano, 1 teaspoon olive oil, and salt to taste. Stir and set aside.

Grill or lightly toast the bread until the surface is barely golden. Drizzle lightly with olive oil. Distribute the cheese among the slices of bread, sprinkling it evenly over the surface but stopping short of the edges of the bread by ½ inch. Place bread slices under a hot broiler for a few seconds, or until the cheese bubbles and is flecked with gold.

Drain the tomato mixture and spoon a little of it over the melted cheese. Serve immediately.

Makes 4 bruschettas.

Bruschetta con Ricotta Fresca

My father loved ricotta, a food from his childhood in Bompietro, a small town in Sicily. He left that life early to go to Palermo to study at the university; but a part of him always remained in his hometown—where a special almond tree spread its branches right into his bedroom window; where prickly-pear cactus ripened to a sugary sweetness in the blazing sun; and where a boy could wander for miles and miles in the countryside.

Fresh ricotta is highly nutritous and lean, with a natural sweetness and a meadow-fresh perfume; its texture ranges from very moist to firm and cake-like.

This bruschetta makes an ideal lunch or afternoon snack, eaten with a few black olives. Or try it for breakfast, sprinkled with sugar and served with fresh fruit.

Fresh ricotta

1 slice country bread

Unsalted butter, optional

Sea salt and coarsely ground black pepper

If the ricotta is very moist, wrap it in several layers of cheesecloth and let drain for at least 30 minutes in a colander.

Lightly toast the bread on both sides. While still warm spread with a little butter, if desired.

Mound the ricotta on the bread and sprinkle with salt and pepper to taste.

Makes 1 bruschetta.

Sweet-Pepper Bruschetta

Peppers, with their bright colors, sweet flavor, and rich, honeyed juices, are a natural topping for bruschetta. Here, finely julienned sautéed red, yellow, and orange peppers are combined with anchovies and capers. Taste the peppers: If they are not as sweet as they should be, add a touch of sugar to them as they cook.

This bruschetta makes a big hit at parties—and the great advantage is that you can cook the peppers a day in advance. Spoon the pepper mixture and juices, either hot or at room temperature, on the bread right before serving.

87

2 tablespoons extra-virgin olive oil

½ medium onion, thinly sliced

3 bell peppers, 1 red, 1 yellow, and 1 orange, cored, seeded, and cut into matchstick strips

Salt

3 anchovies, finely chopped

1 heaping tablespoon capers

4 slices country bread, cut ½ inch thick

2 garlic cloves, peeled and cut in half

Extra-virgin olive oil for drizzling

10 basil leaves, torn into fragments

In the olive oil, sauté the onion over low heat until it wilts, about 5 minutes. Add the pepper strips and salt to taste. Cover and cook over medium heat, stirring occasionally, for about 15 minutes, or until peppers are tender. Off the heat, stir in the anchovies and capers.

Grill or toast the bread on both sides. Rub the hot bread on one side with the cut garlic cloves and drizzle with a few drops of olive oil.

Spoon the pepper mixture and juices over the bread and sprinkle with basil.

Makes 4 bruschettas.

Bruschetta with Spicy Broccoli Topping

Broccoli on bruschetta? Yes, when the broccoli slowly cooks down into a coarse garlicky puree and is mixed with chopped black olives. You won't believe how flavorful this is until you've tried it.

3 tablespoons extra-virgin olive oil

4 garlic cloves, peeled and finely chopped

Pinch hot red pepper flakes

1 pound fresh green broccoli, peeled, stalks and flowerets cut into small pieces

1 cup water

Salt

10 oil-cured black olives, pitted and coarsely chopped

4 slices country bread, each about ¾ inch thick

2 garlic cloves, peeled and cut in half

Extra-virgin olive oil for drizzling

Combine olive oil, garlic, and hot red pepper flakes in a sauté pan and cook over low heat for 2 to 3 minutes, or until the garlic releases its fragrance and becomes opaque. Add the broccoli and stir. Add the water and salt to taste. Cover and cook over medium heat for about 10 minutes, or until the broccoli is very tender.

Uncover the pan, reduce heat to low, and mash broccoli, using the back of a wooden spoon. Continue to cook the broccoli, mashing it with the wooden spoon until the water completely evaporates and the broccoli breaks down into a coarse puree. Stir in the black olives. Keep mixture warm.

Meanwhile, grill or toast the bread. Rub with the cut sides of the garlic cloves and drizzle lightly with olive oil.

Mound the broccoli puree on the bread and, if desired, top with a few drops of olive oil.

Makes 4 bruschettas.

88

Bruschetta with Gigantic Grilled Mushrooms

Grilled mushrooms are so satisfying to eat, like grilled meat, only with light and succulent flesh.

Select 2 big shiitake mushrooms, each as large and round as a saucer. Thick, fleshy caps will maintain their shape and texture when exposed to the intense heat of the grill.

The dark brown mushroom caps, perched atop the grilled bread, have a magical appearance, reminiscent of cool fall days, rain-soaked leaves, and misty forest floors. Serve this bruschetta as a memorable lunch, accompanied by a field salad, or as a first course, followed by a grand stew of vegetables or meats.

2 large shiitake mushrooms

2 garlic cloves, peeled and finely chopped

1 heaping tablespoon finely chopped rosemary, sage, and thyme

Sea salt

Extra-virgin olive oil

2 slices country bread, cut about ¾ inch thick

1 large garlic clove, peeled and cut in half

Trim stems from mushrooms and discard (the stems are extremely fibrous and inedible). Wipe the caps with a damp paper towel. Make 2 or 3 shallow slits in the flesh of each cap.

In a small bowl, combine the herbs, garlic, and salt to taste. Gently stuff the mixture into the slits in the mushrooms. Brush the mushrooms on both sides with olive oil.

Grill the mushrooms until they just begin to soften, turning them once. Overcooking turns shiitakes limp and slimy. When the mushrooms just begin to release some of their juices, they are ready.

Meanwhile, grill the bread on both sides. While still warm, rub one side of each slice of bread with the cut garlic and drizzle with olive oil.

Place a mushroom on top of each slice of bread. Serve immediately.

Makes 2 bruschettas.

90

Capri-Style Bruschetta

When I visited the island of Capri several years ago I tasted a rustic zucchini puree that was used as a pasta sauce. With a few changes—adding mozzarella and hot red pepper flakes—I've transformed the sauce into a creamy, spicy topping for bruschetta.

Although zucchini is delicious when quickly cooked until just tender, this recipe calls for a slow cooking that changes the flavor from light and sweet to rich and savory.

Always select small, firm zucchini, no more than 4 or 5 inches long. Slice larger zucchini lengthwise and scoop out all seeds before cooking.

2 tablespoons extra-virgin olive oil

½ medium onion, finely diced

Pinch hot red pepper flakes, about ¼ teaspoon

½ pound fresh zucchini, trimmed and cut into ½-inch dice

1 tablespoon chopped Italian parsley leaves

2 canned peeled whole tomatoes without additives, chopped, or 2 ripe Roma tomatoes, peeled, seeded, and chopped

Salt

⅓ cup water

3 ounces fresh mozzarella, cut into small dice, about ½ cup

4 thick slices country bread

2 garlic cloves, peeled and cut in half

Extra-virgin olive oil for drizzling

6 basil leaves

Place the olive oil, onion, and hot pepper flakes in a small sauté pan. Cook, covered, over low heat for 10 minutes. Add zucchini and parsley, and stir. Sauté for a few minutes over medium-low heat. Add tomatoes, salt to taste, and water. Stir well. Cook, covered, for about 25 minutes, or until zucchini is very tender and meltingly soft. Mash zucchini using the back of a wooden spoon. Continue to cook until almost all the moisture evaporates. Add the mozzarella and stir until the cheese melts.

Meanwhile, grill or toast the bread on both sides. Rub cut garlic into 1 side of each slice of bread. Drizzle very lightly with olive oil. Spoon the zucchini mixture onto the bread slices. Top with a few drops of olive oil. Tear the basil into fragments and sprinkle over the top. Serve hot.

Makes 4 bruschettas.

92

Bruschetta with Cannellini Beans and Strong Herbs

The creamy texture and mild flavor of cannellini, or white kidney beans, are perfect for strongly herbal rosemary, thyme, and sage. Finely diced red onion lends a zesty crunch to the white bean puree. In summer add diced tomato and basil to the red onion.

This robust bruschetta is a meal in itself when served with a peppery little salad.

1 tablespoon extra-virgin olive oil

1 tablespoon unsalted butter

1 small garlic clove, peeled and finely chopped

1 teaspoon each chopped fresh rosemary, thyme, and sage

Pinch hot red pepper flakes

2 cups cooked cannellini or white beans, or 1 15-ounce can, drained

½ teaspoon sun-dried tomato paste or imported tomato paste

Salt

2 tablespoons finely diced red onion

Freshly ground black pepper

4 slices country bread, cut about ¾ inch thick

Extra-virgin olive oil for drizzling

Place the olive oil, butter, garlic, herbs, and hot red pepper flakes in a medium sauté pan. Cook over low heat for several minutes. Add the beans, tomato paste, and salt to taste. Cook over medium-low heat for about 5 minutes, using a wooden spoon to crush the beans into a coarse puree. Place in a food processor or blender and process until smooth. If the mixture seems dry, add a little water or broth to achieve a creamy texture. Meanwhile, grill or toast the bread on both sides. Drizzle the bread lightly with olive oil.

Spoon the bean puree on the bread and sprinkle with the red onion. Top with a few drops of olive oil.

Makes 4 bruschettas.

93

Bruschetta with Fava Beans and Greens

Dried fava beans are one of the staples of Italy's *cucina rustica*. One way of preparing them is to turn the beans into a coarse puree, served with bitter wild greens. I've used this rustic pairing as a topping for bruschetta. Extra-virgin olive oil, very green and full-flavored, is drizzled over the finished bruschetta—an important final flavoring that elevates and brings together the separate components.

This earthy-looking bruschetta is knife-and-fork food, deeply satisfying served as a main dish along with a glass of rough red wine.

FOR THE BEANS:

1½ cups dried fava beans, about ½ pound

½ teaspoon salt

FOR THE RAPINI:

1 pound rapini, coarse stems trimmed (if rapini are unavailable, use mustard greens, curly endive, or other bitter greens)

Salt

3 tablespoons extra-virgin olive oil

3 garlic cloves, peeled and thinly sliced

FOR THE BRUSCHETTA:

4 slices country bread, cut about ¾ inch thick

2 garlic cloves, peeled and cut in half

Very fruity extra-virgin olive oil for drizzling

Freshly ground black pepper

Put the fava beans in a bowl with ample cold water to cover. Let soak overnight. Drain. Peel the beans. Place the beans in a saucepan with 4½ cups water and ½ teaspoon salt. Cover and bring to a boil. Reduce heat to a steady simmer and cook for 30 minutes. Remove lid and cook until water evaporates and beans break down into a coarse puree, about 30 minutes. Stir often during the last 15 minutes of cooking to prevent scorching the puree. Set aside.

Trim the coarse stalks off the rapini. Peel the tender stems and cut the greens into short lengths. Cook in salted boiling water until tender. Drain well in a colander, pressing down gently with the back of a wooden spoon. Place the olive oil in a medium sauté pan. Add the garlic and sauté for a few minutes over medium-low heat. Add the rapini and stir to coat the greens. Cook over medium-low heat for about 5 minutes, or until all excess moisture evaporates.

Meanwhile, gently reheat the bean puree in a small, heavy saucepan. Grill or toast the bread on both sides until golden brown. Rub one side with the cut garlic cloves and drizzle with olive oil. Mound the bean puree on the bread and top with the greens. Season with salt, coarsely ground black pepper, and a drizzling of olive oil.

Makes 4 bruschettas.

94

Shrimp Bruschetta

This simple recipe captures all the sweet flavor of shrimp accented by garlic and hot red pepper. The time at the stove is minimal—just the few moments it takes to cook the shrimp.

½ pound medium shrimp in the shell

2 tablespoons extra-virgin olive oil

2 garlic cloves, finely chopped

½ teaspoon hot red pepper flakes

1 tablespoon chopped Italian parsley

Salt and freshly ground black pepper

4 slices country bread, cut about ¾ inch thick

2 garlic cloves, peeled and cut in half

4 lemon wedges

Serve as a first course in an all-seafood dinner or as a light main dish. With glasses of cold white wine, it makes a perfect summer offering. You'll feel like you're dining at a trattoria by the sea.

Shell and devein the shrimp. Neatly cut each shrimp into 3 or 4 pieces. Drain well.

Place the olive oil, garlic, and hot red pepper flakes in a small sauté pan. Cook over medium-low heat for 2 to 3 minutes. Add the shrimp and parsley, raise the heat to high, and sauté for 1 to 2 minutes, or until shrimp is just cooked through. Remember the shrimp will continue to cook from the heat retained in the pan. Season with salt and pepper.

Meanwhile, toast the bread on both sides on the grill, under the broiler, or in the toaster. Rub one side of each slice of bread with the cut sides of the garlic cloves.

Arrange the bread slices on a platter and spoon the shrimp and any juices over the bread slices. Serve immediately, garnished with lemon wedges.

Makes 4 bruschettas.

Bruschetta con Frutti di Mare

Here, the "fruits of the sea" include scallops and shrimp bathed in a fresh mint marinade. The cool seafood salad is a seductive contrast to the crisp, hot bruschetta.

½ pound medium shrimp

Salt

½ pound bay scallops, small muscle removed

4 tablespoons extra-virgin olive oil

3 tablespoons lemon juice

1 small garlic clove, peeled and finely chopped

2 teaspoons capers

10 fresh mint leaves, very coarsely chopped

Freshly ground black pepper

4 slices country bread

Extra-virgin olive oil for drizzling

1 ripe but firm Roma tomato, cut into small dice

4 large mint leaves for garnish

Devein the shrimp by making a shallow cut along the outside curve of the shell. If there is a black vein, rinse it away under cold, running water.

Cook shrimp in salted, boiling water for about 2 minutes. Lift out of water with a large Chinese strainer and drain in a colander. When cool, shell and cut each shrimp into 4 neat pieces. Place in a bowl.

While the shrimp is cooling, cook the scallops in the boiling water. After about 2 minutes, or when the scallops are just opaque, drain into a colander. When cool, cut each scallop in half horizontally. Add to the bowl with the shrimp.

Add the olive oil, lemon juice, garlic, capers, and mint to the bowl. Season with salt and pepper. Stir gently. Marinate for about 1 hour at room temperature or for up to 24 hours refrigerated. Bring back to cool room temperature before serving.

Grill the bread until golden brown and drizzle with olive oil.

Add the tomatoes to the salad and stir gently. Correct seasonings. Spoon the salad and juices over the bread. Tear the mint leaves into small pieces and sprinkle over the top. Serve immediately.

Makes 4 bruschettas.

98

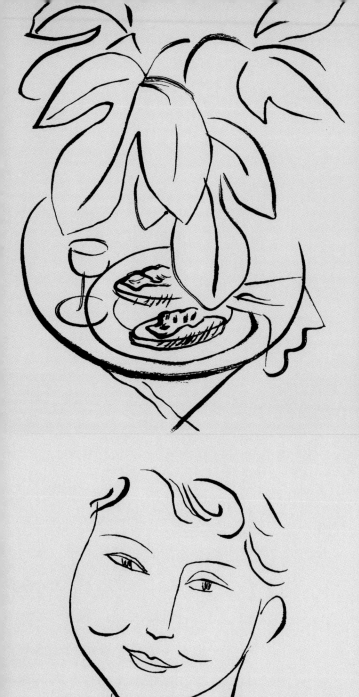
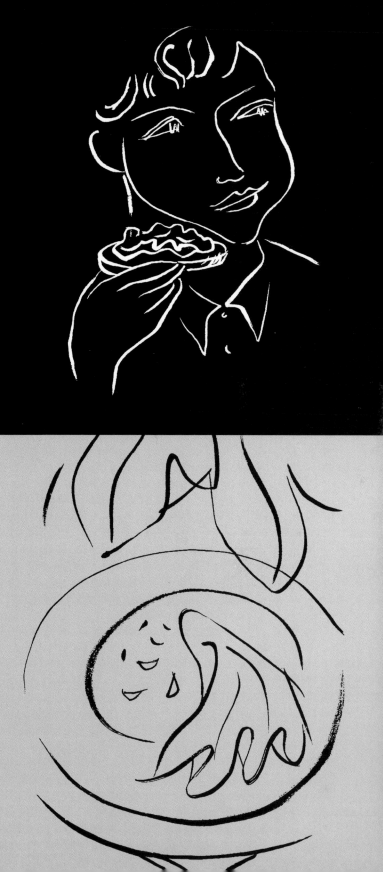

Crostini: Little Toasts

Crostini are small rounds or squares of bread, brushed with olive oil or butter, then lightly toasted in the oven. They are less filling, more delicate versions of bruschetta.

Crostini with savory toppings are traditionally served as antipasti preceding a meal or with aperitifs. You can also enjoy them in a variety of other ways.

Crostini make wonderful snacks: For example, a topping of ricotta, herbs, and shredded carrot satisfies a midmorning appetite—it's healthy, nourishing, and irresistibly good; as an after-school treat, kids love crostini with a pizza-style topping. Serve crostini for brunch, topped with scrambled eggs and capers. A dinner party can start with a dazzling platter of assorted crostini in contrasting colors and textures. These little rounds can also accompany other dishes: crostini with black olive pesto together with slices of fresh marinated mozzarella, or eggplant-topped crostini to accent a main dish of grilled swordfish or tuna.

The following recipes range from a fragrant and colorful topping of diced red and yellow tomatoes and herbs to a stylish spread of avocado and goat cheese. Crostini are easy to make and fun to eat—each one a delightful little biteful of flavor.

Crostini

This is a basic crostini recipe to use as a base for savory toppings.

Select crusty bread with a soft, chewy, and fine-textured crumb. A narrow baguette-type loaf, called a sfilatino, creates little round crostini; loaves in other shapes can be cut into squares or triangles.

Add garlic, hot red pepper flakes, or herbs to the olive oil to flavor the bread if desired.

When serving buffet-style, place the topping in a small bowl or, if very dense, mound directly on a platter and surround with crostini. Guests can help themselves, spooning the topping on their crostini.

See individual recipes for variations on the following recipe.

Extra-virgin olive oil

1 high-quality baguette, about 2 to 3 inches in diameter, sliced a little less than ½ inch thick

Garlic cloves, peeled and cut in half, optional

Slice baguette either straight down or on the diagonal. Brush olive oil on both sides of the bread slices and arrange on a cookie sheet. Place in a 400° oven until bread is lightly golden but not hard-toasted all the way through. If desired, rub one side of each slice of bread with cut garlic cloves. Crostini can be used hot or at room temperature.
Just before serving, spoon on the topping.

Makes about 48 crostini.

102

Crostini alla Checca

If you have a profusion of red and yellow tomatoes ripening in the backyard, this is the recipe you're sure to make over and over. Sweet and fruity, yellow tomatoes add their special flavor and color to this herb-scented raw-tomato topping.

As a final flourish, sprinkle grated cheese over the top of the crostini. Parmesan is more mellow than Pecorino Romano, which has a salty kick. Ricotta salata, when dried for grating, has a creamy taste and a tangy finish.

2 medium yellow tomatoes, about ½ pound

2 medium red tomatoes, about ½ pound

4 tablespoons extra-virgin olive oil

2 garlic cloves, finely chopped

2 tablespoons chopped mint leaves

2 tablespoons chopped basil leaves

1 teaspoon dried Mediterranean oregano, such as Greek oregano

Salt and coarsely ground black pepper

16 thin bread rounds, cut from a high-quality baguette-style loaf

Extra-virgin olive oil for bread

Imported Parmesan, Pecorino Romano, or dried ricotta salata

Core the tomatoes and cut into small dice. Place tomatoes in a bowl. Add the olive oil, garlic, herbs, and salt and pepper to taste. Stir and set aside for an hour to develop the flavors.

Brush both sides of the bread rounds with olive oil. Arrange on a baking sheet. Bake in a 400° oven until crisp and golden. Use bread hot or at room temperature.

Arrange the bread rounds on a serving platter. With a slotted spoon, divide the tomato topping among the crostini. (Drink the leftover juices, a special perk for the cook!) Top with a sprinkling of grated cheese. Serve immediately.

Makes 16 crostini.

103

Avocado and Goat Cheese Crostini

Avocado goes well with tart lemon and lime juice, so it's well matched with tangy, lemony goat cheese. Although this spread sounds incredibly rich, keep in mind that goat cheese is relatively lean and that only one avocado is used for 24 crostini.

These pretty pastel-green crostini make an unusual appetizer to serve with drinks.

1 ripe avocado

5½ ounces goat cheese, softened at room temperature

1 teaspoon extra-virgin olive oil

1 tablespoon lemon juice

Salt and freshly ground pepper

24 thin rounds of bread, cut from a narrow baguette-style loaf

Extra-virgin olive oil for bread

Pit and peel the avocado. Place in a bowl and mash until smooth. Add the goat cheese and drizzle with olive oil, lemon juice, and salt and pepper to taste. Use a fork to mash the ingredients together, stopping before the goat cheese and avocado are completely blended. Taste and correct seasonings. Brush the bread on one side with oil and arrange with the olive oil side up, on a cookie sheet. Bake in a 350° oven for 8 to 10 minutes until crisp but not hard-toasted all the way through. Mound a little avocado-cheese mixture on each piece of bread.

Makes 24 small crostini.

104

Crostini with Black Olive Pesto

Black olive pesto is a dark, lustrous spread with a deep, rich flavor and perfume that are the very essence of the Mediterranean. In this variation, I've added lemon zest and a sprinkling of capers for a simple pesto that is great on crostini. For a summery accent, top the olive pesto with diced tomato and basil. The olives must not be too salty or bitter or the pesto will be too pungent. Taste one first, if possible, before purchase. This is intense, heady stuff, and a little goes a long way!

FOR THE PESTO:

1 cup imported black olives, in brine

Extra-virgin olive oil

1 very small garlic clove, finely chopped

2 teaspoons lemon zest, preferably from an organic lemon

1 tablespoon capers

FOR THE CROSTINI:

12–16 thin bread rounds, cut from a baguette-style loaf

Extra-virgin olive oil

Pit the olives and place in a blender. Process until the olives are either coarse- or fine-textured, depending on preference, adding enough olive oil to make a dense paste. Scrape out of the blender and place in a small bowl. Stir in the lemon zest and capers. Cover tightly and refrigerate until needed. Olive pesto can be made in advance. It keeps for weeks.

To make the crostini, very lightly brush bread rounds with olive oil and arrange on a cookie sheet. Place in a 400° oven until golden on the surface but not hard-toasted all the way through.

Using a teaspoon, spread a little of the black olive pesto on each crostino.

Makes 12–16 crostini.

106

Country Garden Crostini

These delightful little toasts have a fresh-from-the garden taste with their pairing of sweet carrot, fragrant herbs, and creamy ricotta. They make a perfect snack for kids, healthful, light, and nourishing, but are sophisticated enough for adults.

The quality of the ricotta is important: Small companies specializing in Italian cheeses are the most reliable source since large-scale commercial brands tend to be unpleasantly dense and grainy.

6 ounces ricotta (about ¾ cup), drained of excess water

2 teaspoons extra-virgin olive oil

5 large, very fresh basil leaves, chopped

1 tablespoon chopped Italian parsley leaves

2 very thin green onions, finely chopped, or 1 tablespoon snipped chives

1 small sweet carrot, peeled and shredded

Salt and freshly ground black pepper

Unsalted butter, softened at room temperature

12 thin bread rounds, cut from a narrow baguette-style loaf

Wrap ricotta in several layers of cheesecloth and let drain in a colander for at least 30 minutes.

Place ricotta in a bowl and mash with a fork. For a smoother texture you can use a food processor or push ricotta through a fine mesh sieve. Add olive oil and stir well. Add basil, parsley, green onions, and carrot, and season with salt and pepper. Stir again until well blended.

Very lightly butter one side of each bread round. Arrange on a cookie sheet, buttered side up. Bake in a 350° oven for 8 to 10 minutes or until the crostini are crisp but not hard-toasted all the way through.

Use a small spoon to mound the mixture on the warm crostini and serve immediately. The ricotta is also very good on crostini made in advance and served at room temperature.

Makes 12 crostini.

Roasted Eggplant Crostini

The smoky taste of roasted eggplant permeates this creamy crostini topping, with finely diced tomatoes and roasted yellow peppers adding color and crunch. Generously mound the eggplant puree on little rounds of bread and watch them disappear!

Select a firm eggplant with smooth, shiny, deep purple skin; a green stem end indicates freshness.

1 medium eggplant

1 ripe firm yellow bell pepper

1 small red ripe Roma tomato

1 small garlic clove, crushed to a paste

2 tablespoons extra-virgin olive oil

2 tablespoons lemon juice

Salt and freshly ground black pepper

Dried Mediterranean oregano, such as Greek oregano

6 fresh green basil leaves, chopped

12–16 thin bread rounds, cut from a narrow baguette-style loaf

Extra-virgin olive oil for bread

Place the untrimmed eggplant on a gas burner and turn heat to high or place the eggplant under the broiler. Roast the eggplant, turning it until it is blackened on all sides. Use tongs to avoid puncturing the eggplant. After about 10 minutes, the eggplant will look rather deflated and the flesh will be very soft. Carefully transfer the eggplant to a bowl and let cool.

Peel away the blackened skin. If a few specks of charred skin remain, don't worry—they add flavor. Drain the liquid. Transfer the eggplant to a chopping board and chop the flesh into a smooth puree. Place the puree in a clean bowl.

Roast the pepper over a gas flame or under the broiler until it is almost completely blackened. Place in a paper bag and seal tightly. When the pepper is cool enough to handle, rub off the skin. Use paper towels to wipe away any remaining pieces of charred skin. Core and seed the pepper and remove the white membranes. Cut the pepper into narrow strips and then into small dice. Add to the eggplant puree. Core and seed the tomato and cut into small dice. Add to the bowl along with the mashed garlic. Stir the ingredients together. Add olive oil, lemon juice, salt and pepper, and herbs. Stir well. Taste and correct the seasonings.

Brush the bread lightly on both sides with olive oil and arrange on a baking sheet. Place in a 400° oven. Remove the crostini when they are lightly brown, but not hard-toasted all the way through. Transfer to a serving platter.

With a small spoon, mound the eggplant mixture on the crostini. Serve warm or at room temperature. If preparing the crostini in advance, top with the eggplant puree just before serving to prevent the bread from becoming soggy.

Makes 12–16 crostini.

Crostini alla Pizzaiola

Pizza ingredients on a crostini. Simple to prepare for a large gathering and fun to eat!

hot crostini

¼ pound bocconcini, small balls of fresh mozzarella, drained

2 red ripe Roma tomatoes

12 thin rounds of bread, cut from a narrow baguette-style loaf

Extra-virgin olive oil for bread

Salt and freshly ground black pepper

Dried Mediterranean oregano, such as Greek oregano

Extra-virgin olive oil for drizzling

8 fresh green basil leaves, chopped

Cut the bocconcini lengthwise into 12 slices. Drain well on folded tea towels. It is important to drain the mozzarella thoroughly or the crostini will become soggy. Cut each tomato crosswise into 6 slices.

Arrange the bread rounds on a baking sheet. Brush each one lightly with olive oil. Place a slice of mozzarella on each piece of bread. Cover with a slice of tomato. Season with salt and pepper. Sprinkle with oregano and drizzle with a few drops of olive oil.

Place in a 450° oven for about 10 minutes or until the cheese melts and the tomatoes soften. Remove crostini rounds from the oven and transfer them to a serving platter. Sprinkle with the basil. Serve immediately.

109

Makes 12 crostini.

Crostini Topped with Scrambled Eggs, Italian Style

A charming offering for a summer brunch—very special when made with vine-ripened tomatoes and basil fresh from the garden. Arrange the crostini on a platter and sprinkle lavishly with fresh Parmesan.

2 tablespoons unsalted butter

2 garlic cloves, finely chopped

4 large eggs, preferably cage-free, lightly beaten

Salt

1 ripe but firm red Roma tomato, cored and finely diced

1 heaping teaspoon capers

4–5 basil leaves, chopped

Freshly ground black pepper

12–16 thin bread rounds, cut from a narrow baguette-style loaf

2 tablespoons unsalted butter, softened at room temperature

Freshly grated imported Parmesan cheese

Place the butter in a medium sauté pan. Turn the heat to medium low. When the butter melts, add the garlic and cook for 2 to 3 minutes. Add the eggs. Stir slowly over low heat until the eggs start to form small curds. Add the tomato, capers, basil, and black pepper to taste, and stir. Cook briefly, stirring until the small curds are barely firm. Take care not to overcook the eggs.

Meanwhile lightly butter one side of each bread round. Arrange on a baking sheet. Place in a 400° oven. Remove from the oven when the breads are lightly toasted, but before they are hard-toasted all the way through. Mound the scrambled eggs on the bread rounds. Arrange on a platter and sprinkle with Parmesan cheese. Serve warm.

Makes 12–16 crostini.

110

Crostini alla Napoletana

These crostini are a seductive blend of sweet roasted peppers, creamy mozzarella, and tangy anchovy butter.

Use yellow peppers when available—they are intensely sweet and, after roasting, become imbued with a smoky flavor. And I love the way the roasting process leaves brown patches on the golden flesh.

2 ripe yellow bell peppers

¼ pound smoked mozzarella

1 can anchovies in olive oil, drained

2 tablespoons unsalted butter, softened at room temperature

24 thin rounds of bread, cut from a narrow baguette-style loaf

Salt and freshly ground black pepper

Dried Mediterranean oregano, such as Greek oregano

Extra-virgin olive oil

Roast the peppers over a gas flame or under the broiler. Use tongs to turn them frequently until they are charred and blistered, but before they turn ashy. Place the peppers in a paper bag and twist the top closed. Set aside to cool.

Shred the mozzarella on the largest hole of a four-sided grater.

Chop the anchovies to a paste and place in a small bowl. Add the butter and blend well with a fork.

Remove the peppers from the bag and peel them. If possible, do not use water to rinse away the charred skin as water washes away the juices that come to the surface after roasting. Use your fingers to peel away the skin, then use paper towels to wipe away the remaining charred areas. Core the peppers and remove all seeds and membranes. Cut each pepper into 12 neat squares.

Arrange the crostini on a baking sheet and spread lightly with the anchovy butter. Place one pepper square on each piece of bread, peeled side up. Sprinkle the mozzarella over the crostini. Season with salt, pepper, and a little oregano. Dribble a few drops of olive oil over the top.

Place under the broiler briefly, until the cheese just melts and bubbles and is lightly flecked with brown. Serve immediately.

Makes 24 crostini.

112

Crostini with Savory Mushroom Topping

Dried porcini mushrooms infuse cultivated mushrooms with an incredibly deep, wild flavor. Just a small amount is needed to flavor a big batch of mushrooms. Here, they add their bosky flavor to mushrooms sautéed with tomatoes, mint, and anchovies.

Strain the delectable porcini soaking liquid to use in place of beef broth in soups and risotto.

0.7 ounces dried porcini mushrooms

½ pound fresh button or cremini mushrooms

2 tablespoons unsalted butter

1 large garlic clove, finely chopped

3 Roma tomatoes, peeled, seeded and chopped

2 anchovies, packed in olive oil, chopped

2 tablespoons chopped mint leaves, about 3 sprigs

Salt and freshly ground black pepper

12–16 thin rounds of bread, cut from a high-quality narrow baguette-style loaf

About 2 tablespoons unsalted butter, softened at room temperature

Rinse the dried porcini under cold running water. Place them in a small bowl and cover with warm water. Soak for 20 minutes. Lift the porcini out of the soaking liquid, rinse briefly, and drain on paper towels. Reserve soaking liquid for another use. Coarsely chop the porcini and set aside. Wipe the fresh mushrooms clean with damp paper towels. Trim the stems. Thinly slice the mushrooms.

Melt the butter in a medium sauté pan. Add the fresh mushrooms and cook over medium-high heat. When the mushrooms have softened, add the garlic and chopped porcini. Cook for a few more minutes. Add the tomatoes, anchovies, 1 tablespoon of the chopped mint, and salt and pepper to taste. Cook over medium-low heat until the tomatoes thicken into a sauce. Meanwhile, arrange bread rounds on a baking sheet and place in a 400° oven. When lightly golden, remove from oven. Spread butter on one side of each bread round. Top the crostini with the warm mushroom mixture and sprinkle with the remaining mint.

Makes 12–16 crostini.

113

Polenta Triangles with Peppers and Gorgonzola

Here, golden polenta triangles are the base for sautéed sweet pepper strips topped with a dab of Gorgonzola. Colorful and eye-catching, they make ideal appetizers; or serve them as the first course of a dinner party.

Find a source for really fresh *dolce latte* Gorgonzola; much imported Gorgonzola is over-the-hill, a casualty of time and travel. Smell the cheese first; if the odor is very strong, reject it. The Gorgonzola should be a creamy white, veined in blue, not yellowish or brownish and cracked.

1 recipe Fast Polenta (see page 68)

2 tablespoons extra-virgin olive oil

3 large bell peppers, 2 red and 1 yellow, cored, seeded, and cut into thin strips

Salt

Pinch sugar, optional

Extra-virgin olive oil for brushing on polenta

4 ounces imported *dolce latte* Gorgonzola, softened at room temperature

Freshly ground black pepper, optional

Prepare the polenta. Pour the hot polenta into a lightly oiled 1½-quart loaf pan. Let cool, then refrigerate, covered with plastic wrap, until needed. Place the olive oil in a medium sauté pan. Add the peppers and salt to taste. Cook over medium heat, covered, stirring often. If needed, add sugar to taste, from a small pinch to a large pinch, according to sweetness of peppers. Cook until the peppers are tender and soft, about 10 to 15 minutes.

Unmold the polenta and slice into 16 ½-inch slices. If desired, trim polenta to create straight-sided rectangles. Cut each slice diagonally into 2 triangles. Lightly brush polenta on both sides with olive oil and arrange on baking sheets. Place polenta under the broiler, turning once. Cook polenta triangles until crisp on the outside and flecked with brown, about 4 to 5 minutes per side.

Top each triangle with a little of the pepper mixture. Using a teaspoon, top with a little Gorgonzola, about ½ teaspoon per triangle. With the heat off, return polenta triangles to the oven (not under the broiler) for just a moment to warm but not melt the Gorgonzola. Serve immediately.

Makes approximately 32 crostini.

Crostini di Polenta ai Funghi

Get out the knives and forks for this one! Use both wild mushrooms and the cultivated varieties that walk on the wild side such as shiitake, cremini, and portobello mushrooms.

Farmer's markets are a good source for unusual mushrooms. Once I bought a portobello mushroom at a farmer's market that was as large as a dinner plate and at least 2 inches thick. It looked like a mushroom from an enchanted forest and it was enough to produce a pasta sauce for four!

1 recipe Fast Polenta (see page 68)

1½ pounds assorted full-flavored fresh mushrooms, such as shiitake, cremini, portobello, porcini, chanterelles, etc.

4 tablespoons unsalted butter

3 large garlic cloves, peeled and finely chopped

About ¼ teaspoon hot red pepper flakes, or to taste

5 tablespoons chopped Italian parsley

Salt and freshly ground black pepper

Extra-virgin olive oil for polenta

Freshly grated imported Parmesan cheese

Prepare the polenta. Pour into a lightly oiled 1½-quart loaf pan. Let cool, then refrigerate, covered with plastic wrap, until firm.

Wipe the mushrooms clean with damp paper towels. Trim off any hard, fibrous stems. Cut the mushrooms into small pieces.

Place the butter, garlic, and hot red pepper flakes in a large sauté pan. Turn the heat to medium-high and when the butter melts, add all the mushrooms and parsley. Stir well. Cook, uncovered, until the mushrooms are tender and almost all excess moisture evaporates.

Meanwhile, unmold the polenta and cut into 16 ½-inch slices. Cut each slice into 2 rectangles and trim edges. Brush polenta on both sides with olive oil. Grill on both sides until crusty and marked by the grill, about 4 to 5 minutes per side.

Top each slice of polenta with a big spoonful of mushrooms and generously sprinkle with Parmesan.

Makes about 32 crostini.

Sweet Panini

AND BREAD WITH SWEET TOPPINGS

Sweets: Not Just for Dessert

Since bread is such an important part of life in Italy, it seems natural to team it with sweet ingredients as well as savory ones.

I've kept the sweetness in this chapter to a minimum to allow the recipes to be served in different contexts. You'll find bruschettas for breakfast and rustic desserts; crostini to accompany espresso or for elegant late-night snacking; and panini, lightly sweet and nourishing, to tuck into a child's lunch bag. Each recipe highlights a few basic ingredients, among them sweetly fragrant ricotta, bittersweet dark chocolate, perfumed seasonal fruits, and mellow honey.

In a roasted chocolate panino, nutty, somewhat neutral-tasting country bread serves as a foil for intense dark chocolate; lightly sugared fresh fruit bakes on slices of bread until the two merge; simple crostini are topped with a rich spread of mascarpone and cherries; and bread tempers the sweetness of frittata panini flavored with orange marmalade or fig jam.

The recipes are direct and uncomplicated, which gives them their freshness and innocence. But as with all things simple, quality is crucial. Use fully ripened fruits in season and the best ricotta you can find. Only the finest bittersweet chocolate and eggs from cage-free chickens will do. Search out a reliable source for fresh whole nuts, and peel and roast them yourself. The flavor of the ice cream must be pure, not marred by additives or artificial flavors. Above all, the high quality of the bread should set the standard for the other ingredients.

This chapter is dedicated to fun and fancy. The recipes, though touched by sweetness, are incredibly wholesome, since what unites them is bread, earthy and life-sustaining.

Toasted Bittersweet Chocolate Panino

Bread and chocolate is a time-honored Italian tradition—a piece of chocolate and bread or brioche was a popular snack, or *merenda*, that my mother remembers eating as a child in Italy.

2 small slices fine-textured country bread

About ¾ ounce high-quality bittersweet chocolate, roughly ⅜ inch thick, or enough chocolate to cover 1 slice of bread

I've carried on this tradition myself. Here, I've given it an added dimension by toasting a panino of bread and chocolate in the oven until the chocolate melts and the bread is crisp and hot. I love the contrasting flavors of toasted country bread and fragrant melted dark chocolate, and the point at which they merge—the barely sweet chocolate, strong as espresso, melting into the warm, yeasty flavor of bread.

This is a favorite snack of mine. With it I issue two warnings: (1) wait until the panino cools a little or the chocolate, hot as molten lava, will burn your tongue, and 2) you may become addicted!

The amounts of chocolate to use and the measurements are approximate. It's a spontaneous kind of panino made to satisfy a craving, so don't worry about exactness.

Arrange the chocolate on 1 slice of bread, stopping short of the edges by about ½ inch (the chocolate melts so it needs a little extra room). Cover with the other slice of bread.

Place in a 500° oven and toast for about 5 minutes on each side. Use tongs when turning the sandwich over—the chocolate will be somewhat liquid and may drip on you.

The panino is ready when the bread is lightly toasted on both sides and the chocolate melts. Cool briefly before eating.

Makes 1 panino.

Ice Cream Sandwich, Italian Style

I remember eating an ice-cream-and-brioche panino on the small island of Ustica, just off the coast of Sicily. I bought it on the main street—just a few shops and *caffès* and a sleepy little piazza that seemed to turn to liquid in the shimmering heat haze. The ice cream panino tasted cool and refreshing, and it felt good to be in that gelateria, out of the relentless sun.

1 individual brioche

High-quality ice cream, such as vanilla, strawberry, or lemon

Split the brioche in half lengthwise without cutting all the way through. With a big spoon, gently pack the brioche with ice cream. Press the sides of the brioche together to enclose the ice cream in the bread. Serve immediately.

Makes 1 panino.

122

Lemon Frittata and Fig Jam Panino

This panino features a fragrant, lemony frittata nestled between slices of bread spread with butter and honey-sweet fig jam.

I use a luscious fig jam imported from Lebanon. Or you can mash very ripe peeled figs, sweeten with a few drops of honey if necessary, and spread them on the bread instead of jam.

2 eggs, preferably cage-free

2 teaspoons sugar

1 teaspoon finely chopped lemon zest, preferably from an organic lemon

1 tablespoon lemon juice

Tiny pinch salt

1 tablespoon unsalted butter

Unsalted butter, slightly softened

4 large slices country white bread, cut from a large sfilone (each slice should measure about 6 × 3 inches), or 2 large round rolls

Fig jam

Break the eggs into a bowl and beat with a fork. Add the sugar, lemon zest, lemon juice, and salt, and mix well.

Place the butter in an ovenproof sauté pan about 6 inches in diameter. Turn to medium-high and when the butter melts and turns golden, add the egg mixture. Stir until large curds form. When the frittata is firm but the top is still runny, place under a hot broiler until the top is just firm. Turn out the frittata on a plate and let cool. Cut the frittata in half.

Lightly butter 2 slices of bread. Spread with a little fig jam. Top each slice of bread with half of the frittata. Cover with the remaining bread slices.

Makes 2 panini.

124

Orange Marmalade Frittata Panino

A glossy spoonful of bittersweet orange marmalade turns a frittata into a lightly sweet filling for a panino of crusty whole grain bread. A healthy treat for a child's lunch or for breakfast eaten on the run.

Other citrus marmalades such as tangerine, lemon, or mixed citrus would be equally delicious.

1 egg, preferably cage-free

1 teaspoon sugar

1 tablespoon orange marmalade

Tiny pinch salt

1 tablespoon unsalted butter

2 slices Italian-style whole grain bread

Unsalted butter, optional

Break the egg into a small bowl and beat with a fork. Add the sugar, orange marmalade, and salt, and mix until well blended.

Place the butter in an ovenproof sauté pan about 6 inches in diameter and turn the heat to medium high. When the butter just begins to turn a light brown, add the egg mixture. Lower the heat to medium and stir the eggs until curds form. When the frittata is firm on the bottom but still runny on top, slide it under the broiler until just set (overcooking the frittata produces a dry panino).

Meanwhile, lightly butter 1 slice of bread, if desired.

Fold the frittata over like an omelet. Transfer to the buttered slice of bread. Cover with the other bread slice. Serve warm or at room temperature.

Makes 1 panino.

125

Bruschetta with Mascarpone and Raspberries

Mascarpone is a fresh, fluffy white cheese made from sweet cream, often served as a dessert with fruit. In this luscious topping, mascarpone is sprinkled with red and golden raspberries, then drizzled with threads of honey. The bruschetta is at its very best when eaten while the bread is still warm, which lightly melts the mascarpone and honey.

1 slice country bread, about ½ inch thick

Mascarpone

Small handful ripe raspberries

Fragrant honey, such as lavender or orange blossom, at room temperature

Lightly grill or toast the bread. Spread with mascarpone. Top with the raspberries and drizzle a little honey over the top.

Makes 1 bruschetta.

126

Baked Fresh Fruit Bruschetta

This is a combination of sliced bread topped with fresh fruit—like a rustic fruit pie eaten hot from the oven. Make it when soft summer fruits are at their seasonal best.

Unsalted butter

2 slices country bread, day-old or dried out in a low oven

Sugar

1 big juicy nectarine

As the fruit bakes, the edges of the bread toast, the fruit breaks down, and the fruit juices moisten the bread. The hot fruit becomes highly perfumed—like the intensified scents in a summer garden.

Besides nectarines, peaches, apricots, berries, or a combination of fruits can be used. With peaches, peel first after immersing them in hot water for a few seconds.

Serve this bruschetta for breakfast on a summer morning, accompanied by a big cup of *caffè latte*; or as a rustic dessert with small glasses of sweet dessert wine. It also makes a wonderful afternoon snack for children.

Butter the slices of bread and sprinkle lightly with sugar.
Cut the nectarine in half and remove the pit. Slice the fruit and arrange over the bread. Sprinkle only lightly with sugar if the fruit is very sweet. For a more caramelized effect, be more generous with the sugar.
Place the bread on a baking sheet. Bake in a 425° oven for 20 to 25 minutes, or until the fruit softens, the sugar caramelizes a little, and the bread is toasted around the edges. If desired, place under broiler briefly to caramelize the top. Serve immediately.

Makes 2 bruschettas.

128

Strawberry Bruschetta

Southern California strawberries grow in neatly furrowed rows along the coastal road that divides the blue ocean and the rolling hills. In the spring, when the hills become bright yellow with flowering mustard and wild daisies, the strawberries, hidden under their low, leafy green foliage, turn deep red and juicy.

When strawberries are at their peak, I like to serve them sliced and sugared as a topping for bruschetta, a glossy pile atop grilled country bread thickly spread with crunchy walnut butter.

1 basket ripe strawberries

Sugar for strawberries

4 slices country bread

4 tablespoons unsalted butter, softened

2 teaspoons sugar

4 tablespoons chopped walnuts, coarsely crushed in a mortar and pestle

Stem and slice strawberries. Sprinkle with sugar to taste and stir gently. The amount of sugar depends on the sweetness of the berries. Set aside. Lightly grill or toast the bread. Spread with the walnut butter. Top with the berries and any juices that form.

Makes 4 bruschettas.

130

Bruschetta with Cannoli Cream

Highly nutritious, light, fresh, and fragrant ricotta is used as the filling for cannoli, a famous Sicilian dessert. Here, this classic filling is flavored with orange, bittersweet chocolate, and toasted almonds, and tops bruschetta. Serve as a rustic dessert, a healthful afternoon snack, or for breakfast with a foamy cup of cappuccino.

3 tablespoons raw unpeeled almonds

8 ounces ricotta, preferably made by a small, artisan-style Italian cheese company

1 tablespoon sugar

Finely chopped zest from ½ small orange, preferably organic

2 tablespoons bittersweet chocolate, chopped into small pieces

4 thick slices country bread

Unsalted butter, optional

To peel the almonds, immerse them in boiling water very briefly, less than a minute. Lift out with a slotted spoon and place on a clean dish towel. When the almonds are cool enough to handle, squeeze them between your fingers to pop off the skins. Dry the almonds. Spread them on a cookie sheet and toast in a 350° oven for 10 to 15 minutes, or until the almonds are lightly golden brown. Remove from the oven and when cool, coarsely chop.

Put the ricotta in a food processor and blend until smooth. Or push the ricotta through a fine sieve to remove any lumps. Transfer ricotta to a bowl and add the almonds, sugar, orange zest, and chocolate. Stir well. The mixture can be made several hours in advance. Cover and refrigerate until needed.

Toast the bread slices until golden brown on the outside but soft within. Lightly butter the slices if desired. Spread with the ricotta mixture.

Makes 4 bruschettas.

131

Bruschetta with Ricotta and Fresh Fig Spread

My mother's fig tree is my source for the sweetest figs imaginable. Picked when they are fully ripe, their flesh is like jam, as sweet as if they had been drenched in honey.

3 ounces best-quality ricotta (about ⅓ cup), drained

2–3 small ripe figs

Honey or sugar to taste, optional

1 large slice country bread

Unsalted butter, optional

1 fig, thinly sliced, for garnish

A few mint leaves

Combined with fresh ricotta, figs make an inspired bruschetta spread, with the fruit supplying all the sweetness. If the figs are less than perfectly ripe, add a little sugar or honey as needed.

This makes a lovely breakfast to eat in a summer garden along with a big cup of strong cappuccino or a glass of fresh orange juice.

Wrap the ricotta in 4 or 5 layers of cheesecloth to absorb excess moisture. Set aside in a colander for at least 30 minutes.

Stem and peel the figs. Mash them well with a fork.

Remove the ricotta from the cheesecloth and combine with the figs. Mix together until you have a rough puree; a little roughness is part of its charm. Add some honey or sugar if needed.

Lightly toast the bread. If desired, spread a small amount of butter on the hot bread. Top with the fig-ricotta spread. Layer fig slices over the ricotta. Sprinkle with mint, tearing each leaf into 2 or 3 pieces.

Makes 1 bruschetta.

Crostini with Mascarpone and Cherries

These dainty little morsels are amazingly simple to prepare and taste absolutely extraordinary.

Mascarpone is sugared and spiked with clear cherry maraschino liqueur, spread on warm crostini, then topped with brandied cherries. With each bite the cherries release their juices, merge with the mascarpone, and soak into the bread.

Please don't even think of using artificially colored maraschino cherries, sold in jars for mixed drinks; they bear no relationship to real marinated cherries and are completely inappropriate for this dish! Either make your own (see following recipe) or purchase from a specialty food shop.

4 ounces mascarpone

1–2 tablespoons sugar

1 teaspoon maraschino liqueur or kirsch

Unsalted butter

16 small rounds of bread, ½-inch thick, cut from a narrow baguette-style loaf, or 16 small rounds of brioche

Sugar for crostini

½–¾ cup drained, pitted brandied cherries, about 32 to 48

In a small bowl, combine the mascarpone, sugar, and liqueur. Stir well. Cover with plastic wrap and refrigerate for about 30 minutes.
Lightly butter and sugar the bread rounds and arrange on a baking sheet. Toast the crostini at 400° until they are crisp on the outside but soft inside. Remove the mascarpone cream from the refrigerator. Spread the cream on the crostini. Top each bread round with 2 or 3 cherries. Serve soon after assembling them.

Makes 16 crostini.

134

Cherries in Cherry Brandy

These luscious brandied cherries are simple to prepare. With a cherry pitter—an inexpensive, indispensable gadget—you can pit a pound of cherries in under 5 minutes!

1 pound fresh cherries, pitted

¾ cup sugar

¾ cup kirsch

Place cherries, sugar, and brandy in a small saucepan and bring to a boil. Transfer to a bowl and let cool. Spoon cherries and juices into a tall jar and cover tightly. Store in a dark place for at least 2 days before using.

Makes 2 cups.

Crostini al *Caffè* e Cacao

Refined and not too sweet, these diminutive bread rounds are topped with a creamy blend of mascarpone cheese, espresso, cocoa, and sugar—reminiscent of tiramisù. Serve as an unusual dessert accompanied by little cups of espresso or by champagne. These crostini make wonderfully indulgent afternoon or midnight snacks. If possible, prepare several hours in advance, as the flavor of the mascarpone spread deepens the longer it rests.

4 ounces mascarpone

1 teaspoon finely ground espresso

1 teaspoon Dutch-process cocoa

1 tablespoon sugar or to taste

About 12 small rounds of bread, sliced ½ inch thick, cut from a baguette-style loaf, or 12 small rounds of brioche

Unsalted butter

Cocoa for sprinkling on top of the crostini

Place the mascarpone in a small bowl. Add the espresso, cocoa, and sugar. Stir well to blend thoroughly. Cover with plastic wrap and refrigerate for at least 30 minutes or overnight to develop flavors. Remove from refrigerator a few minutes before serving.

Place the bread rounds on a baking sheet and toast them in a 350° oven until lightly golden on the outside but soft within.

If desired, lightly butter the crostini. Then, using a knife, spread the mascarpone mixture on the crostini, smoothing it into low mounds. Dust the tops very lightly with cocoa.

Makes 12 crostini.

Index

Page numbers in color refer to color photographs.

139

140

141

142

143

144